PROMISES OF OUR CIRCLES:

A Proleptic Journey to Kingdom Economics & Kingdom Leadership

by

Lamont Robinson

authorHOUSE

AuthorHouse™
1663 Liberty Drive
Bloomington, IN 47403
www.authorhouse.com
Phone: 1 (800) 839-8640

Published by AuthorHouse 11/23/2015

ISBN: 978-1-4259-4144-4 (sc)

Print information available on the last page.

Any people depicted in stock imagery provided by Thinkstock are models,
and such images are being used for illustrative purposes only.
Certain stock imagery © Thinkstock.

This book is printed on acid-free paper.

Because of the dynamic nature of the Internet, any web addresses or links contained in this book may have changed
since publication and may no longer be valid. The views expressed in this work are solely those of the author and do
not necessarily reflect the views of the publisher, and the publisher hereby disclaims any responsibility for them.

Scriptural quotations are taken from The Word: The Bible from 26 Translations, Mathis
Publishers, Inc., Gulfport, MS 39506-6685. All rights reserved.

Scriptural quotations are taken also from The Amplified Bible Copyright 1954, 1958, 1964, 1965,
1987 by The Lockman Foundation and Zondervan Corporation: All rights reserved.

Scriptural quotations taken from The Nelson Study Bible, copyright 1997 by Thomas Nelson, Inc. Used by permission.

DEDICATION

This book is dedicated to my mom Beatrice Mooney Robinson who taught me how to persevere and to never give up on my dreams and never take life for granted for each and every breathe of life is important. Through your example of tender love you taught me how to love again and how to be a servant by serving you and others more than myself. I've learned that my challenges don't compare to what you continue to overcome daily in your pain which you carry lightly and for that momma I am grateful and can't thank you enough. Thank you mom for sharing your grace and peace with me which makes serving you even easier.

The operations of the spirit, the wind (the ruach) goes to the south and circles back around and whirl to the north ; it swirls and twirls about continually, and on the Lord's horizontal circuit the circles of the wind flows in cycles until it return again. To my son "LaLa" Lamont LaMarcus Robinson for remaining happy from day one and understanding during those times of temporary separations; thanks to you for maintaining a connection in our relationship that was never disconnected and for that I am most appreciative. Continue to mature in the spirit cause our future is indeed bright.

To my entire family and friends thank you for all of your encouragement to continue on and the continued patience to wait when on countless occasions I told you all at different times that I was done when I thought I was. Now, I can finally say it is done!

In fond Remembrance to the greatest dad in the world
Mr. David L. Robinson Sr.

Table of Contents

About The Author

It is with deep, sincere humility and gratitude that my lord and his sweet holy spirit chose me to present to the reading audience this serendipitous work. The hidden treasures of Wisdom I've discovered within the Word of God have graciously been bestowed upon me, which I've hid in my heart to present in these pages specifically the biblical and spiritual aspects of kingdom leadership and kingdom economics. Then, I further give a comprehensive introduction and analogy of Satan's world debt system; in order to conclusively distinguish between the fake debt system of the world and the parallel properties of God's system of kingdom economics. My hope and prayer is that this book and the format presented will remove all preconceived teaching of the learned and enlightenment to the unlearned.

If we are spiritually receptive to listening with divinely open ears and swift in discerning the kingdom dimension (seeing how to create ubiquitous phenomena) within this unique kingdom message of the written and living Word of God through this book, it will open up the mysteries of kingdom economics to you and provide completeness that will quicken your heart, mind, and soul with solutions to the missing links of our lives. You will experience the living Word and it will manifest and reveal to you God's invisible thoughts the same way it has continually done for me in this period of my life. Again, it is with deep, sincere gratitude that my Lord God-Adonai has deepened my relationship through my obsession with scriptures, namely, the written word of God. During this period of 6 years other levels of preparations occurred that led to physical restraints, emotional lamentations, psychological renewal and a mental reconfiguration of my thought processes which I describe as holy trauma. All these conditions mentioned were startling experiences that happened simultaneously as my natural outlook on life was ruptured and old thinking patterns started an eroding separation from the worldly culture of complexities and fragmentation and sin; resulting in great compassion for the human suffering in the world. In addition to the profound disorientation from a way of life I ignorantly assumed had value; instead, had seemed to offer nothing but hardship and pain.

This new awareness made relating to that old life and the world difficulties increasingly boring. However, it also made my new mental outlook quite challenging, isolating and intriguing. The continuous process of contextualizing the word of God into larger expressions of meaning specifically defined for me a compressed context of kingdom leadership and kingdom economics. I actually repudiated my transformational experiences of kingdom thinking because it continued to force me to think outside of the boxes and my comfort zones. During these volatile times the context of kingdom thinking was still obscure and abstract to me as I continued the painstaking effort of trying to understand how Adonai wanted to manifest his covenant promises and blessings for me and His true leaders.

It wasn't until a mental shift occurred from looking at the kingdom from a traditional religious teaching that the written word became the spoken word of God. The breakthrough was like early morning dew upon the fresh new buds of a vast landscape upon the mental consciousness of my mind. Kingdom listening is by far the most important attributes one can develop in understanding and listening to the still soft voice of the Holy Spirit. This form of solitude and isolation created in me a mental atmosphere of divine listening that simplified the letter of the word of God. As a result, the spirit that's inherent to the letter or text started pouring out its wisdom to me by means of continuous visualization and revelation that led to an accelerated rate of receptivity. Not just hearing the word of God, but seeing the word of God. It was here when my apprehension and awareness of the prophetic word grew within my inner man; that the fresh revelation of the wisdom and mysteries of God erupted upon my renewed mentality with such divine intensity that a zeal and endearing passion forced me to engage at the table of grace. This feeding by the Holy Spirit resembles a baby boy in a feeding chair for his first time.

He doesn't know what to expect except that he's extremely hungry and his mother puts the prepared food of apple sauce, mashed potatoes with gravy and butter, tender baby peas and mashed carrots, plus some cookies and cake and ice cream with Jell-O, vanilla pudding along with a jelly sandwich, oat meal, and a bottle of milk and orange juice to wash it all down.

Kingdom thinking will enlarge your hearts and renew the capacities of your minds as it has my mind. Kingdom thinking will empower you to practice the mind of Christ in comprehensively understanding the content of the scriptures in reference to Kingdom economics. The simplicity of the living word in your life will create such a thirst within your souls that as a king or queen you will learn how to allocate kingdom resources and manifests the promises of the kingdom on earth. This is the wisdom of heaven. The treasures of unseen dimension of wealth laid up for you.

No accomplishment of my past could not have prepared me except the day I received the Lord Jesus Christ in my life. However, there must come a moment in ones salvation where Adonai (Lord as a ruler in the earth, Adonai Jehovah as Lord God the headship and overlord, as owner and proprietor) will touch the lives of millions who hunger for the accurate knowledge of His will and purpose of Gods plan in preparing a people that is prepared to overcome this world system through the application of Kingdom economics that is manifested practically through kingdom leadership and their kingdom structures. To make known, show forth and shower his promises and blessings on the true leaders of the kingdom. Kingdom leaders who can utilize and bless the various aspects of the body of Christ and bring forth a continuous harvest of leaders will impact the church through the principles of kingdom economics. It is for this reason; that the honor and the glory of Christ and the living word of God may be manifested and magnified in the world through kingdom leaders.

To share your examples of leadership as a leader, any impacting experiences economically among the youth, college student, and young professional adults, or any kingdom insights the Lord may have graced you with according to the Word of God. We would love to hear from you if you wish to participate at higher levels of leadership: by impacting accelerated change within the next generation of kingdom leaders (generation "X") and start to address the serious issues of closing the economic gap and social divides within the family unit.

To accomplish these huge objectives outside of just discussing the concepts of kingdom leadership and kingdom economics; people need a system they could actually understand how to apply these principles to; but more importantly, a system that can also manifest and demonstrate the promises and blessings according to the content of this book. Understanding these major benefits of the system create a level of anticipation and excitement for the people that actually brings the principles of this book alive; allowing them to introduce the biblical connection between kingdom economics and leadership into the business world today on a greater scale than ever before.

For $27.00 you can purchase your copy of Promises Of Our Circles at our book site: www.kingsn24712.org; visit our blog: Spiritual Kingship/ Where are the Kings at www.kingsn24712.org/blog (on the right side of map site under the Blogroll category and click on Promises Of Our Circles connecting you back to the Book website: www.kingsn24712.org). We expect our readership to be extremely excited about the awesome comprehensiveness of its content and the spiritual qualities and abstract nature of the book. The blog is an extension of the book and are concise excerpts concerning the dynamic phenomena once the kingships are spiritually activated. The blog depicts the majestic aspects of certain graphs and the most predominant royal features of divine intensity that is fused into the king's leadership and its simultaneous royal features of this ubiquitous phenomenon and how divine intensity is inherently infused through the activity of the multiplicity of kings (the masters integrators of assemblies) and into all of their various kingdom leadership structures (multitude of peoples or nations) as one simultaneous accession of integrations. The process of actuation is unique to this type of kingdom integration because it is all performed and accelerated by the operation of the spirit as a ubiquitous phenomenon that only occurs with the implementation of the DNA of Christ. This ubiquitous phenomenon is the DNA of Christ, a prophetic blueprint which exist beyond this book and blog, awaits to become a practical and personal phenomenon for that small percentage of our readership as serious prospects. Those who wants to apply this kingdom blueprint into kingdom plans of action. The clearer your understanding of this kingdom blueprint increases the simpler its kingdom application becomes; and consequently, your thinking becomes less obscure and the abstract aspects of your kingdom promises can now start to become more of an actual reality. Today it is our hope, goal and primary purpose at Lamrob Enterprises Marketing Groups to demonstrate in the marketplace these two correlated and powerful principles (kingdom economics and kingdom leadership) beyond the pages of this book Promises of Our Circles as a manifested reality in the lives of kingdom leaders.

Consequently, if you gleam the vision and glean the promises of your spiritual kingship for yourselves and see what these types of kingdom platforms, its structures of simultaneous integrations and a dynamic capital system that is designed to produce these type of phenomenal results for you in the marketplace. Then you too can allow this simple system of continuous activity to assist you in activating the divine heritage of your spiritual kingship and achieve your higher purpose in life. This is the fulfilling consummation and magnifying activity within the DNA of Christ. Then you can become empowered with others in bringing forth collectively the promises in the never ending circles for many generations. This culminating state that was once eclipsed by a latent state of ignorance and inactivity can now be specifically utilized through our countless circles of spiritually activated kingships with such explosive force bringing renewed hope and regeneration into the business activities of kingdom leaders and restoration in the lives of their kingdom leaderships through the administration of wealth redistribution. This king's decree is the heritage that is laid up with power for you the kings to manifest this power in their kingdom on an epic scale as real and ubiquitous phenomena throughout the marketplace.

Now that you know you are spiritual kings with eternity in your hearts, spiritual kings with its spiritual kingdom at your hands and your past and future promises being here with you right now is the start of your proleptic journey. The only question now is where are the spiritual kings and their spiritual kingships and leadership? Can you believe that there exist a unique opportunity to activate your spiritual destiny in this economy for a more accelerated and simple demonstration of these two very powerful kingdom principles. Act now by seizing your heritage (the DNA of Christ) and learn how to apply them to our eccentric and definite plan of action. This blueprint will not only create divine intensity, which is the consummated work of the spirit for you in the marketplace; but it will also activate an accelerated inheritance by magnifying and redistributing its inherent legacy of promises, throughout the multitude of spiritual kingships nation wide. Kingdom teaching package #1 is available for a minimal cost you can access at level #1 which includes 3D graphic with the audio tutorials that will show you how to extract the essential principles and resources that will accelerate the learning process needed for kingdom thinking and action. For more information visit our blog www.kingsn24712.org /blog or e-mail us at:lamrob24712@gmail.com or promisesofourcircles.com give us your feedback, and follow us on Facebook, U-tube and twitter.

For a minimum cost to that select few from our serious readership, those who are the doers, the movers and shakers, the seasoned young professionals, christians who wants more than just religion, or anyone who has a dream and don't want to be just average but do not have the right vehicle. Than, if this is you and you have identified with your spiritual kingship, then you may qualify to access 2 systems for the price of one. With access codes plus your specific strategic materials and much much more. Email our private email at: 4reallittleones@bww.com for qualified prospects leave your contact information, your interest level of integration and get started on your present future journey today. While these simple strategy and business system have worked for others, we can not guarantee that the principles in this book can become applicable or work for you. We hope however, that the biblical ideals presented here will help you in developing profitable businesses and leadership organizations, according to the 2 kingdom principles laid out in this book promises of our circles.

About The Book- Main Points

1. Promises of Our Circles will show you the Mystery of the church or the bride in relations to the kingdom or the "DNA of Christ":

- This book gives one the general comparison between the kingdom of God or the kingdom of the Son of man: His dear Son Christ Jesus (now beyond the government of theocracy as we knew it then), and the world's financial debt system and political leadership which "we the sovereign people" of God depends on more today than His kingdom principles; you will also learn how "we the people" through the adoption as sons can take claim of Christ's heritage today, which is what we were predestined to then, and is still today, while in the world but not of it. As spiritual kings in this invisible economy within the democracy of God, His spiritual kings who is anonymous and autonomous are progressively becoming more impactful and relevant again in the marketplace.
- You'll learn the various meaning of circle: a man lifetime or generations, posterities within a generation, inheritance passed on within a generation, encompass or compass every side, bind or knit, a circuit, observe feasts or festivities and celebrations, to crown, royalty, protection, no beginning and ending, Alpha and Omega, Author and Finisher, Infinite and Eternal.
- Learn the process of transitioning the pastoral office in order to utilize the king's office.

2. This book will also show the unity of kingdom structure needed to sustain kingdom leadership and the strategies needed to support kingdom economics:

- You'll learn the 3 levels of the king's inheritance: **KOTP**-(kingdom of the priest), **KOTK-H** (kingdom of the kings and heirs), **KOTG**-(kingdom of the gentiles); political leadership vs. kingdom leadership
- You'll learn how "the Fullness of Christ" is paramount to establishing freedom & material dominion over debt & poverty

3. You will learn how to manifest divine intensity within the Body of Christ as it relates to time:

- Learn how to accelerate your spiritual knowledge base Plus Accelerated growth of your covenant promises
- Learn how to translate harvest cycles into business cycles that restores overcoming blessings

PREFACE

1) The words, phrases, sentences, definitions, notes, and author names of references that are in **bold** type act asquick locators, pointing the reader to the kingdom theme within the chapters.

2) The biblical verses that are in **bold** fonts only, is the focal point of the main kingdom theme of each chapter. The **bold** scriptural passages refers mostly to the new testament and is treated in their proleptic (future now) state; or in other words, the kingdom is present now. While the **bold** *italic* scriptural passages refers to the old testament, its treatment pertains to the prophetic (past now) of this kingdom scenario and what has already been fulfilled in the kingdom that is at hand today. Both treatments are designed to show the interconnected similarities they have in relations to the main kingdom theme of its past and future as a ubiquitous presence.

3) The underlined scriptural passages reveals to us the momentous spiritual imports of our decreed promises and blessings that could be fulfilled today with the proper medium and financial vehicle. The combined compositions of all the scriptural verses especially through the 3 promise phases of unity, work, and time; have been specifically setup to accelerate and intensify our readers comprehensive interconnectedness with the kingdom content of that section of each chapter. With this synthesize subject matter, our readers will relate better as kings in Christ kingdom according to this kingdom context. Eventually, these targeted scriptures layout the kingdom scenario of each section of that promise phase; so that the content can be subjectively contextualized into a three dimensional (past future now) kingdom mentality, manifested both in your minds and lives, as you progress through all 9 promise phases and their figure explanations of this book.

The 3 levels of the king's inheritance is represented by three acronyms: the **KOTP**-(kingdom of the priest), the **KOTK-H**-(kingdom of the kings and heirs), the **KOTG**-(kingdom of the gentiles) and this book reveals the leadership aspects of God from the past and compares it to the political leadership of today; in addition, to showing how diametrically oppose their economic systems are to one another.

Worship Acknowledgement

I can not help but express the blessedness of this new found/*ashrey* or happinesses, the plurality of His majesty: which means the great glories and great graces of His majesty. The joy in Jehovah is greater than the actual joy of the inheritance pouring out (on his people) continuously. **El Shaddai** is God Almighty who sees all and knows all putting His omnipresence into operations. He is the Giver of abundance the all bountiful. **Jehovah Jireh** my provider who is omnipresent performing all things for his people as **Elyon,** the possessor of heaven and earth, who divide the nations their inheritance and dispenses the blessings to those in the earth.

Jehovah Elohim of heaven, through and before times eternal, is the God of Abraham, the God of Isaac, and the God of Jacob. The Vine through which both the king line and the priest line flows. This Branch, which sprouts out from the Rod of Jesse, is the Root, the offspring, the seed of David and his kingdom, which is not of this world.

Therefore, **this Christ**, who is from the seed of Abraham, is in fact Christ who was before Abraham was and consequently is the same incorruptible seed that is in you. In short, this **Prince of Peace**, the incorruptible seed that is in you; is greater than he, the prince of this world. That is another reason why he is worthy of my declaration and my acknowledgement and my due honor and my written praise because He is the blessed and only potentate. The **Prince of the kings** of the earth and above all that, He is **King of Kings and Lords of Lords** of those who are redeemed both in heaven and on earth and is now in Christ, My God.

The truth of the matter is what the Spirit revealed to king David then, and what he said about his Son who was not yet born. Saying, "the **LORD** said to my **Lord**", which denotes that **Jehovah** Himself asked **Adonai** who, by the way, sits on two thrones. Presently, at the right hand of His Father's throne where his enemies are set as a footstool by **Jehovah Himself.** And secondly, **Adonai** on his own throne will himself put all enemies under his feet. Above all this, is to be shown my inheritance though the life-giving revelation of God was promised to me and spoken of by **Elohim** though the Godhead. I can rest assured and place my trust in the fact that **Jehovah-Shammah** is he who is there, and is He who is always with me. And is He who can not lie!

God the Son/the Eternal/, and infinite, and the Beginning and Ending, is He Who was and is, and is to come. This is my God who is my inheritance. **Jah** is

Jehovah as having "Become" my salvation. He Who Is, and was and is to come. I Am in Hebrew is **Ehyeh**. I Am that I Am is '**Ehyeh Asher 'Ehyeh**". ___*This is He, the I Am Who I Am and What I Am and WILL BE WHAT I WILL BE or BECOME. I AM THE I AM THAT IS WHO I AM. I AM THE SOVEREIGN GOD*___ supreme Lord of the universe. Who fills all in all according to the needs of those with who He is in covenant relations with me?

Jehovah is the same God in covenant relationship with his creation. He who is <u>Savior</u>, <u>Redeemer</u>, <u>Deliverer, the Strengthener, Comforter, Advocator</u>, All in All, is forever and forever. The omnipresent God Who will never leave you nor forsake you. This is my spiritual praise and worship to you God.

El in spirit **Emmanuel** is God within. Spiritually speaking, we are made in the image of **Elohim** and in the likeness of the Godhead, being **God the Father**, (my spiritual relationship-as his creation), the **Son of Man**, the Word, the Alpha and Omega. This is **Jesus Christ** the humbled, **Messiah** the Anointed with all dominion in the earth with great power and reign. **Christ Jesus** the exalted One, the **Son of God** the heir of all things, the **High Priest and King** upon his throne whose kingdom is not of this world but is throughout the eternities of the eternities.

Finally, I must give thanks to God and Christ for the third part of the trinity, the Holy Spirit. where I am the heir of the promise having received the spirit of the wisdom and the understanding of their spirit through the Mind of Christ. I now, see the promises of my inheritance. I now see the operations of the Holy Spirit and his gifts and graces he has bestowed upon me as an heir. I am empowered now to integrate his operations into the democracy of God, although his works are not yet, fully made applicable in my life and within the whole family of God, including the church in due season it will. I envision the seasons and see the full manifestation of your covenant promises that will glorify the Godhead of the trinity and produce freedoms and bring forth blessings to the Body of Christ.

I am excited with great expectation for the work that's ahead. Manifesting the will and purpose of God's plan of restitution of his kingdom leaders and the restoration of their heritage and inheritance that is past on from all the generations of the ages, to the present generations of today and to the generations of the future. I thank you **Jehovah-Elahay** (the Lord my God) and **Jehovah-Eloheenu** (the Lord our God).

And finally I thank you for revealing the understanding of kingdom leadership, kingdom inheritance, strategies and the Messianic structures that produces "unity" which produces covenant promises and increase business activity. I thank you for providing the leadership of the 10,000,000 Partnered Kings United

Initiatives. I thank you for Lam Rob Enterprises Marketing Groups designed to integrate the invisible economy-your people back into the profit structure of your economy. Above all of this, and far more important to me, in order that I can bless you Lord and that You get the honor and the glory due You from me and this leadership. I must claim this gift and use it to bless others, so that others can bless others.

Overview Explanation of Figures 1- 9

It is easier to see 3 dimensionally or three-fold than to think 3 dimensionally or three-fold. Have you ever heard the cliché that a picture can say a 1000 words? Well in our case the diagrams and graphs of our figures can do the same thing and have an even greater mental impact; especially, from a present now viewpoint rather than a prophetic (past to the present) perspective or proleptic (future to the present) perspective indicated in *figures 1 and 8*. The 2 basic theme associated with the 9 *figures* is the vertical and horizontal relationship to one another. This activity includes combinations of interrelatedness and organizational performance across any and all 12 horizontal circles collectively.

The position between both graphs and diagrams are juxtapose or set in parallel arrangements; in a attempt, to show the reader their correlative activities between the various combinations and what is happening simultaneously resembling a ubiquitous phenomenon. That is why it is imperative and your prerogative for our readers who plan on applying these kingdom principles to take the time to study and comprehend the explanations of the 9 *figures*; especially since *figures 6 and 9* are connected in real time; and because they are transitional graphs, they will help you understand how to transcend your mental disconnect when you see the connection of the two phases of both figures are actually operating at the same time for you. The 2 basic theme associated with the 9 figures is the vertical or spiritual dimension of our spiritual kingships as spiritual kings. We are preordained and justified by the ubiquitous king lines of Christ and the eternal kingship of Melchizedek; which parallels the horizontal dimension of our physical king line Judah, Jesus, and reciprocated full circle back to Christ, the DNA of Christ as our present now blueprint for today. However, to simplify your understanding the most important thing to remember is that all kingdom activities; including all of its consummate combinations and its phases occurs in circle 42, rather ubiquitous or not with circle 42 and circle 1 and circle 1000 all being the same!

This activity is magnified in any and across all 12 circles horizontally with tens of billion (1,000,000,000) of circles vertically integrated in and through those 12 circles throughout a 1000 generations all happening by the DNA of Christ within circle 42. When the sovereign power of God is used by His kings; then our authority instantly becomes manifestations of divine intensity when we introduce the DNA of Christ into the free enterprise systems of the marketplace.

How great will it be when you the king actually realize the overcoming power that is developing within you, and your circle, and in your lifetime and in your generation of circles. Understanding these accelerations and integrations produced by the operations of the spirit are supernatural activities occurring within the DNA of Christ for you the king. This action represents the divine intensity that is compressed in each and every circle and is potentially made available only for spiritual kings to exercise their authority in circle 42 indicative to promise phase 3 in *figure 9*. Consequently, creating a ubiquitous phenomenon in circle 42 that produces ever expanding circles of spiritually activated kingships; for a wealth transfer and disbursement of a 10,000% divine compensation payout that is quickly dispersed throughout these kingdom leadership structures. These consummating promise phases are galvanizing forces that are all encompassing demonstrations of Kingdom economics and kingdom leadership, being the promises of our circles. Reference *figure 9* graph explanation.

There're 9 figures in this book which are made up of collated graphs, with *figures 1, 3, and 8* being the primary figures of all the figures. *Figure 1* consists primarily of 2-phase 4 graphs with both dealing with **integration**: the 1st phase 4 graph is **project 27: divine grace intensified** and it is on the left while the 2nd phase 4 graph, **the present now** graph is on the right. These 2 graphs in *figure 1* represents a collection of 3 other graphs as seen in *figure 3 and figure 8*. Now, *figure 3 and figure 8* shows the individual break down of the 2-phase 4 graphs, which are made up of 3 phases. The project 27: divine grace intensified graph has 2 phases plus a structural diagram which reads clockwise starting with phase 1: the king line of Christ (vertically) and the 12 tribes (horizontally). Project 4/ phase 3 represent the influx of Gentile nations (KOTG) that is received by phase 1: the king line of Christ; with promise phase 3 KOTG diagram showing the structural layout of both phase 1 and project 4/phase 3. Promise phase 3 structures represents the magnified activity in a circle as 10k or 10,000 x 12 which is 1M or one million (1,000,000) across 12 circles received from circle 42 to circle 41. The present now graphs in *figure 8* have 3 promise phases that moves in a clockwise direction also. Promise phase 1 is **unity**, promise phase 2 is **work**, promise phase 3 is **time** and the last, promise phase 4 is **integration**.

The 8 graphs of *figures 3 and 8* have been collated to visually help my readers develop a comprehensive understanding of their inheritance and to be able to compare to a degree, some of the distinguishing properties associated with their heritage. Further elaboration in the remaining 6 figures will show more combinations of ***integration*** from the 8 graphs of *figures 3 and 8* as you progress further in the promise phases of the book.

The DNA of Christ is adorned with an heritage that is arrayed with spiritual qualities resembling jewels of rubies, pearls, emeralds, and diamonds; which also represents various levels of spiritual knowledge needed in acquiring our kingly heritage of old today. Attaining this priceless inheritance entails hidden dimensions of wealth; that has been transmuted into its financial equivalent and transposed into a ubiquitous platform. Consequently; when these modernized platform is accessed by the spiritual kings, then we become the medium, through which the power of the Holy Spirit and its ubiquitous operation can work through. To produce phenomenal phases of wealth redistribution first to the multiplicity of spiritual kings and their kingdom leadership structures of phase one. Through this medium, the spiritual kings of today, who develop these kingdom structures are like peculiar treasuries or stored cities. They will act as depositories and treasuries for a copious deposit of redistributed wealth; in which God can deposit into perpetually as these structures expand and multiply. The kings now have the capacity to actuate and administrate the kingdom wealth of God's economy to an innumerable multitude throughout the nations in our generations today.

The eternal purpose of the DNA of Christ is to become an manifest expression of the true essence of kingdom economics to discover and reestablish the treasure troves of unlimited treasuries and depositories. The economic magnitude equates today financially to a divine coronation for the entire DNA of Christ, with a compensation package of a 10,000% payout indicative to the business cycles of *figures 4 and 7.* This modernized economic activity is comparable to the copious seasonal or holy time cycles of the 7 harvest feasts of old represented in *figures 6 and 9.*

It is important to understand that every activity has all previously occurred within circle 41 and was first extended across the 12 horizontal circles. Represented as 12 disciples and the last generation of Jesus. Transitioning and duplicating itself into the tens of thousand's (10K) and the millions (1M) of circles shown in *figures 3, 6* and *9* as the consummation of the DNA of Christ *figure 1.* This is the immediate annex of Jesus when transformed into the DNA of Christ, like a mustard seed which is transformed into a forest to bring forth its fruit. Like wise, when circle 41 is transformed into circle 42, the DNA of Christ became superimposed as an powerful and dynamic force, with the activity of acceleration exercised upon all generations, while being magnified simultaneously throughout the multitude of nations. This is where the apex of eternity enters the moments of our reality for the 1,000,000,000's of circles: starting the genesis of a ubiquitous phenomenon for its kingdom leadership, and instantly becoming the quintessential demonstration of kingdom economics all within circle 42. In summary, Christ supersedes Jesus because Jesus dealt with the present past then while in the earth. But is now, through Christ's eternal and royal existence; bringing forth in our present future now, the royal fullness of His times as our appointed times now. In our royal lives Christ reawakens us as His (multiplicity of spiritual kings) over comers in the marketplace today. Where it would seem like 1 day with God's Christ would be like a 1000 years.

PHASE 4: COMPOUND INTERRELATIONS OF SIMULTANEOUS UNITY OF KOTK-H, KOTP, KOTG & ACCELERATED INTEGRATION OF PROMISE PHASES 1 UNITY, 2 WORKS, & 3 TIMES

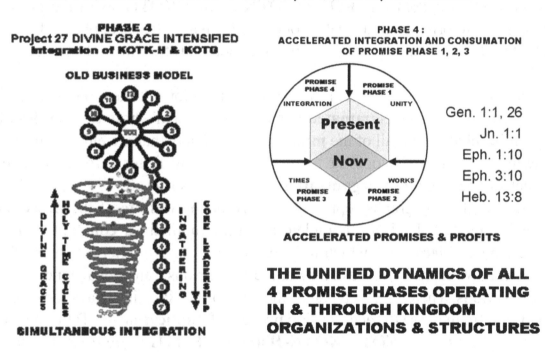

Figure 1

FIGURE 1 GRAPH EXPLANATION

The simultaneous and dual aspects of both phase 4 graphs points specifically to generating the accelerating processes of **acceleration** through simultaneous **integrations** within the various levels of the **kingdom structures**. The **KOTK-H** which is the most important component of the kingdom but is over shadowed today by the **KOTP;** which is suppose to be the smallest aspect to the kingdom. It is actually preventing the largest aspect of the kingdom the **KOTG** from entering into the promises of the **KOTK-H**. *Figure 1* symbolizes the **intensified sovereignty** of the **kings' kingdom** and represents the divergence of the threefold facets of the kingdom (the **KOTP, KOTK-H, and KOTG**) with the primary focus being to bring forth the called out ones from all 3 levels of phases 1, 2, and 3; that will come from the kingdom organization and structures of Christ shown in *figure 4*.

Here is a brief description of the primary operations of the 2 phase 4 graphs in *figure 1*. It is the **consummated activities** of Adonai's **holy time cycles** (the 3 promise phases) and all of the **munificent blessings** that are either constantly flowing or constantly looking to increase its flow faster throughout every aspect of the **kingdom organization** and all its structures. In *figure 1*, the 2 promise phase 4 graphs represent the **present now state** of the **process of integration-POI.** Both are complete and they maintain a **constant state** of increasing **accelerations;** which in turn produces for the other 3 phases of the **present now** graphs in *figure 8*, a dynamic and various transitional conditions of **accelerations**. Therefore, as a result, the state of the **POI** is always looking for conditions to increase the acceleration **process of duplication-POD** through any of the 3 phases of the **KOTP, KOTK-H and the KOTG** in *figure 8*. The faster the **POD** through the promise phases of 1, 2 and 3 the greater the **POI**. Therefore, the feed back process through the phases (the **integration**-leader and structure development, **transition**-promises and blessings and **duplication**-accelerated distribution of the 1st two) of the 2 phase 4 graphs creates simultaneous states of **accelerations, that accelerates the acceleration process** back to the promise phase 4 state.

But when the 2 conditions of the **POI** and **POD** exist simultaneously, the characteristics of the 2 phase 4 graphs feed back process shifts and accelerate instantly into higher states of **simultaneous** and **accelerated integrations;** which in turn, produces **increase dimensions of divine intensity** throughout the 3 interrelated structures and their phases in *figure 3*. Phase 4 graph of project 27 is specifically suited to provide the **intensity** needed to **magnify** all the phases between both phase 4 states. The **POD-process of duplication, because it magnifies the integration** of both **POI** and **POD** will continually transition and accelerate these processes into higher dimensions throughout all the **graphs**, the corresponding **diagrams** and the **circles** in *figure 4-7* and *9*. All the diagrams reveal additional dimensions to the graphs horizontal and vertical relationship. They give illustrated action between the **POI** and the **POD** and the various causes and effects acting upon one another within the kingdom structures. Divine grace is the dimension behind kingdom economics and when it is intensified, by increasing the accelerating process of acceleration and magnifying simultaneously the process of integration, it will draw kingdom leaders and produces kingdom organizations and leadership for national and global impact. It will protect against Satan's modus operandi, the overshadowing lie, all that the interludes reveal through this book and resistance to his opposition to our 3 promise phases.

The 3 Promise Phases Prelude

The **three promise phases**: *unity, work and time* sequentially compounds with the next phase until the climatic phase of integration in promise phase 4. However; although all 3 phases are interdependent of each other, they are at the same time intangibly interconnected with each other distinct and varied uniqueness for a quintessential manifestation of the DNA of Christ and the copious profusion of its hidden dimensions of wealth into circle 42. The symbolic and ubiquitous characteristics of each promise phase culminates into promise phase 4 integration; which is simultaneously transposed into the other phase 4: old business model of figure 3 completing the circle around the isometric three sided cube represented in *figure 8*. The economy of grace and its perfect law of freedom is also representative of the kingdom of God. It is the main theme of the apocalyptic symbols used in the bible of Revelation 21. It is through symbolism that we can understand the spiritual completeness and the excellence in revealing the hidden dimensions of wealth to the present generation in circle 42. These symbols will help expand the reader's scope as kingdom leaders through the maturation process, towards applying some duplicatable resemblance of this perfection and how to administer the business aspects of kingdom economics.

The **3 promise phases** have their identity which is characterized by its own symbolization and each symbolic characteristic is distinctively assigned to each promise phase. The 3 promise phases must be seen collectively as 1 continuous activity of multiple integrations and accelerations, all within itself as indicated by the 2-phase 4 graphs in *figure 1*. The activity of the **4 present now graphs** in *figure 8* is all inclusive too, but is also connected and complementary to the other graphs in *figure 4, 5, and 9*.

The 1st symbol representing (promise phase 1: unity) the marriage feast of one unified humanity the bride of Christ circle 42 being in covenant engagement to the DNA of Christ circle 41. It relates to the perfect and complete oneness **(the promise of our circles)** of the 12 tribes, the foundational wall that are garnished with the priceless jewels with its inherent spiritual qualities. This activity happens within each individual person or circle in the 3 dimensional relationships of the 12 tribes collectively; as mentioned in Rev. 21 which by the way is Gods' manifested government on earth.

The 2nd symbol representing the (*promise* phase 2: work)) is the **four squared city** or **"cube"**. These 3 phases makes up and represents the total dimensions of the **cube**. Although, the **cube** or the 4 **present now graphs** in *figure 8* is placed in the *time* chapter it is designated to **all** 3 Promise Phases chapters. It symbolizes all the consummated **works** of the operations of the spirit and comprises the 3 relationships (*unity, work, and time*) of divine activities in the kingdom of God. Although the dimensions of the (isometric) cube appear to be limited, confined and enclosed within the area of the 3 plane cube, it's the all encompassing **circle** of Christ who gives this symbolic cube its ubiquitous characteristic. The 3 planes or facets of the isometric **cube** are perpendicularly connected (at 3 right angles or 3 spatial axes) to one another. A plane having two dimensions: with breadth being the vertical window of time and length or the horizontal window being that of unity on earth. Therefore, we can see throughout scriptures that this is the basic foundation for manifesting kingdom economics and any move of God though the operations of the Spirit will create a single unified symmetry of God's holy time cycles, which is uniquely inherent only to kingdom economics.

The 3rd symbol is the **New Jerusalem**. In (*Promise* phase 3: time) the (**New Jerusalem**) is the designated symbol representing the spiritual, not material landscape or country of Jerusalem as our inheritance. Freedom and largeness is the dimensional characteristic of this promise phase: time. In addition to the freedom aspect, another aspect to this dimension is the newness found in New Jerusalem, the numerical restoration and qualitative renewal that is greater than ones previous experience of the past; which is why cube or present now graphs in *figure 8* are placed in chapter 3. Promise phase 3: *time* is the productive, resultant, or action session. It's the most elaborate and is designated to the characteristic of the (**New Jerusalem**). Its dimensional characteristic relates to the geometrical and arithmetical operations of the spirit and its expressed works in time and space. The **time** phase is also dynamic not static like the **unity and work** phase is. The **time** phase displays and set forth in an instant the accelerated characteristics of the prophetic decree and its inherent messianic promises exquisitely manifested throughout the structural framework of the (**DNA** of the **bride of Christ**) represented by the *promise phase: unity*. In essence, all three promise phase: *unity, work and time* epitomizes the ornamentation of the prophetic decree that is proportionate to kingdom faith and the messianic promises that are proportionate to applied faith and is divinely implanted and realized from within.

All this symbolism provides a beautiful metaphoric image which helps enlightens the inward state of our spiritual consciousness. Our internal awareness of the kingdom of God will become a real experience when we can externally demonstrate it as a reality and not just symbolic. Therefore, in order for this beautiful presentation to become a reality it's required that our hope be attached to the mustard seed of faith and bound by the truth that all the promises and blessings of the kingdom of God is present now.

At the beginning of the 3 promise phases is a promise phase prelude. The **promise phase** prelude for *promise phase 1: Unity* is the "promise prelude: Wisdom"; the promise phase prelude for *promise phase2: Work* is "Filling the **king's** treasuries; and "Harvesting the spiritual moments of now" is the promise phase prelude for *promise phase 3: Time*. These 3 preludes are in-depth exegeses revealing critical mental truths, pertaining to the spiritual and material aspects, of kingdom economics and kingdom leadership. These 3 preludes prepare the mind of the leader to receive the main content of the **3 promise phases. The preludes clears away and seals** the leaders mind once the wisdom is introduced; thereby, offsetting the negative conditions presented in the corresponding interludes of the **3 promise phase chapters**.

Finally, *figures 2* and *5* are the graphs for the **interludes**. The interludes are presented as an interruption in the middle sections of each promise phase chapter. The three **interludes** are designed to identify the negative effects and their underlining conditions from the past and clarify the consequential impact on present or future situations. They also reveal critical facts and turning points based on some historic crisis that normally have gone unnoticed or forgotten. **The interludes expresses** the antitype to the prelude and how these erroneous conditions are diametrically opposed against the three promise phase of *unity, work and time* as they relate to the consummating forces of kingdom laws of leadership and economics (overcoming promises, covenant blessings) and their distribution within the unified structural leadership of the many sided church through Christ Jesus.

So, in concluding, let me reiterate, the most important point to remember is that every symbolism of the kingdom: its symbols, structures, and types; even time and space; action, work, and their results in the present now are to be seen in its completeness and perfect state **now** through the eyes of Christ. This runs throughout the 3 promise phases of the book and with the visual assistance of the *9 figures* the reader will develop Christ view and look beyond the limited antitypes of the **3 interludes**, which presently seems to foreshadow the Oneness of Christ and His kingdom, to see your own perfection and be your own completeness in Christ and his kingdom which is in fact your kingdom too, being inside you as a king through Christ!

SIN KEEPS THE CHURCH & MULTITUDE STAGNANT & OFF TARGET OF GOD'S ACCURATE KNOWLEDGE & PURPOSE

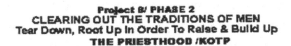

Project 8/ PHASE 2
CLEARING OUT THE TRADITIONS OF MEN
Tear Down, Root Up In Order To Raise & Build Up
THE PRIESTHOOD /KOTP

THE 2ND PHASE: KOTP
TRIBE OF LEVI: THE PRIESTHOOD

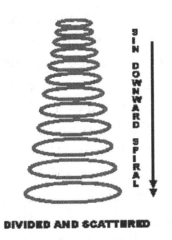

DIVIDED AND SCATTERED

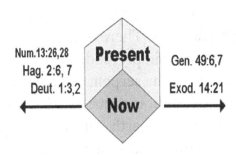

No Inheritance, Possessions;
Divided and Scatter

THE DICHOTOMY OF THE OPERATIONS OF ANTICHRIST

Figure 2

FIGURE 2 GRAPH EXPLANATION

The graphs in *figure 2* show how willful sin based on ignorance keeps the church which is after the priesthood of Aaron stagnant and the multitude of God's chosen off target and to the left according to his accurate knowledge, desired purpose and decreed promises for the kings; which by the way is also compounded by the inability to see what is noble and morally good or evil and diametrically opposed to the development of kingdom leadership and kingdom economics. The graphs of *figures 2 and 5* are the operations of antichrist and the division of the KOTP representing all the interludes.

SATAN'S Modus Operandi
Opposition to the 3 Promise Phases

It would be extremely advantageous and profitable to start at the beginning even before Adam and Eve sinned in the garden. This powerful but brief identification of Satan's **dichotomy** will explain the premise of why and where all the unidentifiable sins originated from, regardless of all the problems, conditions or circumstances which most of the world focuses on; what's crooked can't be straightened out. Therefore, sin isn't repented of, confessed, and forsaken. We must start by simply understanding though Jesus teachings he exposes for us the lineage of the serpent seed and the underlying sin and evil spirits behind its modus operandi. In Genesis 1:1, 2 we see that in the beginning God created the heavens and the earth. On the seventh day he found his work to be very good and beautiful. He also on the seventh day finished his work and had rested from his work. God also blessed the seventh day and sanctified it; so likewise, we too should rest from all our work through Christ who is our daily Sabbath. However, it is stated in Genesis 1: 2 - the earth was without form, and void and darkness was upon the face of the deep. When you first read verse 2 it seems that God created the earth without form or wasted (which in Hebrew is **tohu va bohu denoting that the earth was not created tohu or wasted or empty but that it had become that way**). Upon farther study we see the lie and expose the Truth. In other words, the Truth being that all of God's creation he "saw that it was good". God did not create the earth tohu va bohu but that **Lucifer** the morning star, who like lightning had fallen from heaven and was cast down to earth weakening nations had become "the god of this world".

The disruption or (ruin) of the world is a condition that refers to man and as a result, in like manner, man seems devoted to corruption and the outcome his operations always ruinous. This condition stems from the word katabole and it means "over throw", "cast out" or "cast down" to the ground that is cursed with the serpent. [Ref. Isa.14:12]

From the beginning of Genesis that old serpent, the liar and deceiver grew into a dragon in the book of Revelation. From biblical history, we can see though one of Jesus most important metaphor how he identified more than just the inherent problems of society's dilemmas and its conditions of that time; but more importantly, Jesus revealed the underlying cause behind these erroneous and accepted conditions that permeates throughout every aspect of our lives. In Rev.2:9 and 3:9 Christ identified the synagogue of Satan and his subtle methods and myriad operations though the first prophecy in Gen.3:15 of the serpent seed. The Word also identified for us the metamorphosis concerning the serpent seed of Satan was grafted into the earthly religious culture of that day through the priesthood of Aaron. Eventually, the religious leadership of Aaron was transmuted into the grandiose priesthood of the Sanhendrin Council and its many forms of institutional sects and synagogues after Jerusalem temples had been destroyed by its captors. The Kenites was a primary agent because they were descendents of the first murderer Cain who was also the son of the murderer the devil. "**They are of their father the devil and the lust (works) of their father they must do**" were utilized as Satan's agents then. Between that point on they have murdered the prophets, and inevitably they showed their ultimate disdain when "**they cried out the more exceedingly to crucify Jesus**" and today in this generation you find that evil spirit crying out even more exceedingly.

But kingdom leaders must never forget (after Satan works is finished) the consummation of Christ kingdom is yet to come in the seventh and final trump. However, Satan transverse a dividing line between kingship and priesthood introduced the occasion for his dichotomies to become revived through the priesthood of Aaron and have transitioned ever since. That's why the compact wisdom of Jesus becomes distinctly clear as he reveals the lineage of Christ as both king and priest as one in him and not of the tainted Levitical priesthood of Aaron; but both from the kingship of Judah! When the people of God look beyond the lie, which is covered over with a multitude of sins, then the royal heritage of Christ's kingdom can be seen in the spirit from within us and the lie of Satan's serpent seed is cleared away from around us. So until than, and inevitably in vain the commonplace thought of the world is looking at and dependant upon the dominance of the political left and secular religion of the so called right for support that is slowly disintegrating right from under them and we wonder why the divide.

Where is the balance found between these two antithetical extremes of the serpent seed in Genesis that grew into the Dragon in Revelation? Unfortunately, there can't be any balance between these twin dangers until Christ return. Until then there is work to do and that is kingdom leadership must prepare themselves first as an example to be world on how to over come and thereby lead others by example. In the Humor of Christ, **Elton Trueblood** expounds on the two leavens that of Herod and the Pharisees "how the possible alternative to a particular error may be another error. Therefore, since the possibilities of evil are plural, we must be aware of moving from one to another. That the fundamental dangers were not single, but is multiple.

Finally, until Christ kingdom is established in the minds of kingdom leaders they will not experience His covenant promises and overcoming blessings to live a Life of Truth that sets men free. Until then, we will continue to go though the sufferings, persecutions, trails and tribulations that Satan's kingdom inevitably produces. We should be maturing more in Christ through His kingdom here on earth is the only way to over come the world debt system. Until Jesus return, Christ's kingdom leaders are commissioned to be doing the Word; this will prevent biblical illiteracy in the church and the ignorance of the world about Satan. But if not, we have no choice but continually choose between two evils, the dictatorship of government on the right and false teaching of religion on the left.

So unfortunately, the commonplace thought of the world is entrapped and dependant upon the economic dominance of the political right. In addition to the silence submission of secular religion (the so called Right) has unknowingly entrapped its congregations. By complying with the Liar, (that Old Serpent) and its ruinous lies as an accepted way of life the church leadership is exposing themselves and their following to the associated corruption leading to apostasy or "a falling away".

The church leadership then (the scribes Pharisees and the Sadducees) always condemned Jesus for all the good that he shown in liberating the captives and all the miracles he performed for the masses. This is Satan's modus operandi or method of operation to kill, steal and destroy all while remaining hidden. But fortunately for us, Satan's motive operandi was not to pass by the perceptive and penetrating insight of Christ; thereby, labeling and identifying the deception even for generations to come that haven't been born yet. Only though his Father's word could those who understand this truth could understand how to become free.

We as kingdom leaders need to understand why Jesus identified them as being not from Abraham seed as they (the church) had unknowingly thought; but you are from the serpent seed, of your father the Devil (as the murderer and the liar) being the father of the lie; and from the beginning the evil works your father have done you must do also. What an eye opening statement for those who seek the truth. They must also finish the evil works that their fathers before them started. We the kings must also finish the good works that Jesus finished, that Christ is continuing to finish through His multiplicity of kings.

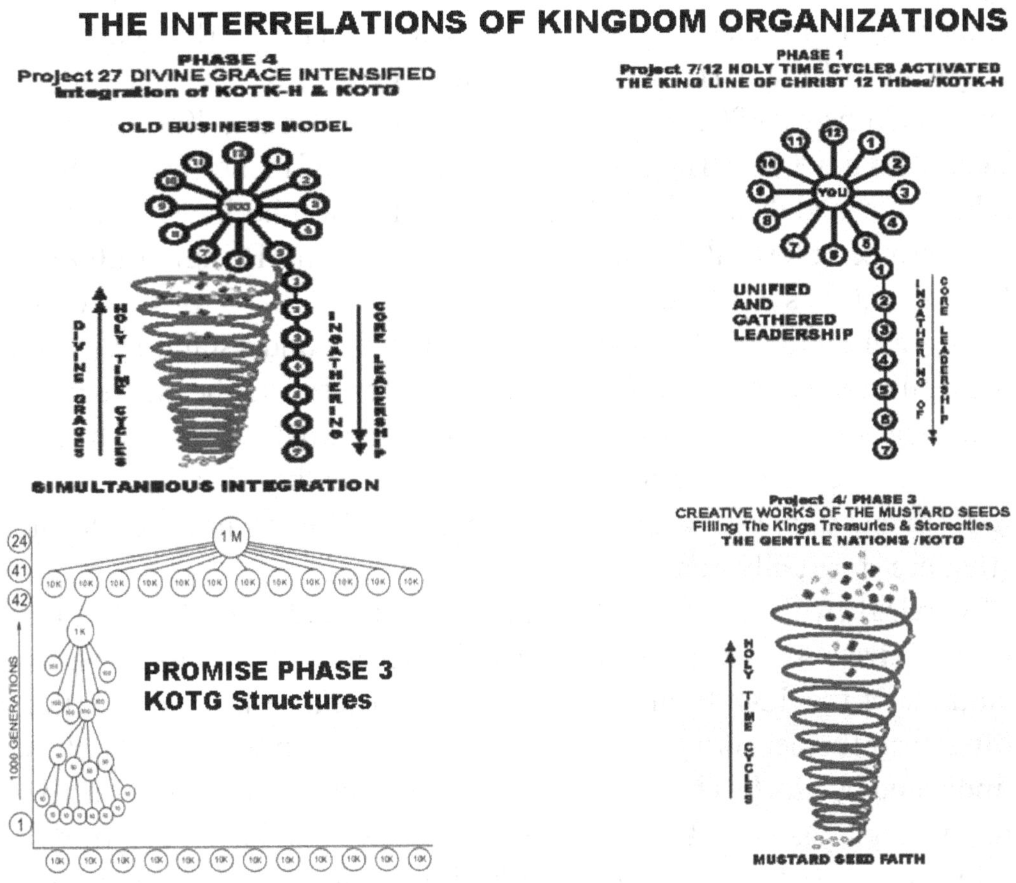

THE INTERRELATIONS OF KINGDOM ORGANIZATIONS

Figure 3

FIGURE 3 GRAPH EXPLANATION

The 4 graphics in *figures 3 and 8* are expanded veiws of figure 1 showing the interrelations and their correlations with *figures 6 and 9*. The consummation of divine grace and accelerated integration starts and finish at project 27/phase 4 moving clockwise through both project 7/12 phase 1 and project 4 phase 3 being the culmination of phases 1 and 3. The project numbers explains the spiritual and biblical significance in the graph's title, and the activity necessary to achieve the promised phase of our king's heritage through the DNA of Christ. For example the number 27 means divine intensity and is necessary to overcome the world's financial system.

In *figures 3* of project 7/12, the 12 circles or 12 tribes of the body of Christ is the leadership represented by the 12 circles of phase 1. Ref. pages 70-74 for the keywords of the various types of characteristics of Christ's kings 932: (5207 sons, 3423 heirs, 4862 joint heirs, 4829 co-participant, 4909 co-laborers etc.). Those who have construed the logical meaning of mentally seizing one's spiritual kingship, and then possess the promises of their inheritance will become masters of the assemblies within the realms their kingdoms. Bringing 1,000,000's (1k/1,000's of 10,000's + 10's of 1000's x 50's + 10's of 100's) of believers and non-believers alike as kings. For a more comprehensive understanding reference *figure 9* graph explanation. The 7 vertical circles represents the entire physical and now the spiritual king line (the multiplicity of spiritual kings) of Christ with His kings receiving their inheritance His 12 tribes or the 12 circles. Instantly bringing forth and duplicating Christ's example of fathering multi-dimensional leaders that are spiritually mature.

The 7 vertical circles are not just connected to any and all of the 12-12 circles in *figure 7* of **circle 41**, but is also connected vertically as well as horizontally to any and all of the 12-10k circles throughout the entire kingdom structure; descending even further into these organizational structures of the 3rd phase of KOTG indicated by **circle 42**. The purpose of the diagram in *figure 4* is to give the reader a simple visual of kingdom business cycles that have been translated historically from a complicated type of holy time cycles/feast harvests from the past. The business cycle here resembles **compound percentages** (4%, 25%, 33%, 10,000% payout, etc.) that are not related to debt or attached to it; but are in fact, compound blessings of the 3 phases, which are symbolic of the 30, 60,100 fold harvest.

It is easier to see 3 dimensionally or three-fold than to think 3 dimensionally or three-fold. Have you ever heard the cliche that a picture can say a 1000 words? However, in our case the diagrams and graphs of our *figures* can do the same thing and have an even greater mental impact; especially, from a present now viewpoint rather than a prophetic (past) or proleptic (future) perspective. That is why it is imperative and your prerogative for our readers who plan on applying these kingdom principles to take the time to study and comprehend the explanations of the 9 *figures*. The 2 basic themes associated with the 9 *figures* is the vertical or spiritual dimension of our spiritual kingships as spiritual kings; which we were preordained to and justified by the ubiquitous spiritual king lines of Melchizedek to Christ. This spiritual lineage shifts simultaneously within the entire DNA of Christ. The correlative shifts extends horizontally and vertically through all circles reciprocally between circle 41 and circle 42 until they both becomes one. However; the vertical lineage now shift into a ubiquitous manifestation, transitioning across all horizontal circles coming full circle reciprocally as a magnification and glorification of Christ. For the spiritual kings this is our blueprint for today's ubiquitous manifestations of our promises.

Once seized, our phenomenal heritage can now descend and ascend reciprocally and seamlessly through circles 24 and 41 and 42 for a 1000 generations eternally. From the generation of Abraham circle 1, through the generations of king David to his son, the King, Jesus the Christ and His 12 disciples the 41st generation as circle 41; which today makes up the entire physical heritage and spiritual king line of Jesus now embodied in Christ; and although our inheritance seems to be laid up in reserve, it is still superimposed upon this last generation as circle 42. Circle 42 represents the 42nd generation (ref. page 115), and is illustrated by the 7 vertical circles: the entire spiritual in gathering (from the past, present and future for a 1,000 generation) of the core line of kings (the multiplicity of spiritual kings) and their 12 circles of kingdom leaders shown in *figures 1,3,4, 6 and 7*. This was the physical king line of Jesus. However, as His heirs, sons; the most interesting and powerful aspect is what happens during the transition from circle 41, when the physical king line of Jesus is superimposed through the spirit of Christ upon us this last generation. Forever, even to the unborn; this inheritance is instantly available today to those who chooses to be His adopted sons and daughters as joint heirs and heirs to His Father, who now have the great opportunity to seize their inheritance. This generation of young professional adults is where all this ubiquitous activities of wealth redistribution occurs. It is simultaneously dispensed vertically and horizontally throughout all generations within circle 42 (shown in every *figure* except *figures 2 and 8*) when certain conditions are met. These expansive and progressive levels within these three transitional phases (represented by the transitional graphs of *figures 6 and 9*, ref. page 41) depicts the totality (*Figure 1 and this figure 3*) of the 2n1 phenomenon (ref. page 131.1, represented by *figures 4 and 7*) by the divine ubiquitous acts of the churches: [when circle 1 as circle 24 (represented as *figures 2, and 5*) transitions to becomes integrated into circle 41 (*figures 7 and 4*), all while being superimposed upon billions 1,000,000,000 of circles all within circle 42 (figures 6 and 9)]. This completes the 2n1 process within the DNA of Christ. Ref. pages 18.1, pages 37,41; pages 69-74, and pages 115, 130-132.

This activity is magnified in any circle and across all 12 circles horizontally with tens of billion (1,000,000,000) of circles vertically integrated in and through those 12 circles throughout a 1000 generations all happening by the DNA of

Christ within circle 42. When the sovereign power of God is used by His kings; then our authority instantly becomes a manifestation of divine intensity, which is recognized when we introduce the prophetic blueprint of the DNA of Christ into the free enterprise systems of the marketplace. Thereby, producing a ubiquitous phenomenon that is inherent to the DNA of Christ.

Kingdom leadership and kingdom economics are the 2 quintessential principles infused, as the perfect blueprint and embodiment in the DNA of Christ, as the democracy of the Godhead (The Father, The Son, and The Holy Spirit). However, as aesthetically pleasing it is to the mental and emotional senses, all this spiritual perfection is by no means the totality of its essence; or even the central focal point, today it mostly remains an abstract entity locked up in both the past and future. But, the true essence is when we, the multiplicity of spiritual kings can produce and set forth the complete expression of this divine state in the human experience. Exercising our power through the ubiquitous operation of the spirit, we can manifest an event, that will become a ubiquitous phenomenon through 1000's of generations as a white field harvest experience.

Hence, the wisdom of the kings, which is not limited to the boundaries of the ages. But is for unfolding the historic canopy of Christ Jesus grasping His prophetic blueprint and sovereign heritage from both His past and future abstract entity to our present manifestation now. The only way to close the gap between these two dilemma and transcend their limitation; is through the expressed enactment of the DNA of Christ. We as kings must become the integrators that mediates between the extremes of these disconnects; thereby, bridging the gaps and bringing forth our foreknown covenant promises and pouring out our overcoming blessings upon phase 1 and phase 3 as shown in *figures 3, 6, and 9.*

When this occurs, then the glory will be to God when the apple of His eye (the DNA of Christ) is magnified. God who walks on the vaults of heaven will immediately deposit the intensified riches of His grace and glory, creating ubiquitous phenomena of white field harvests throughout the entire structures in the DNA of Christ. But only for those kings who wish to exercise their spiritual kingship will they become the intermediaries in the midst of the earth. Through the DNA of Christ the kingdom will seem to be present here on earth, with the grace of God working His eternal purpose for His spiritual kings as a present now experience.

KINGDOM IS PRESENT - NOW ON EARTH

PROMISE PHASE 1: UNITY
Promise Prelude: Wisdom

She, **wisdom** was there in eternity since before all the **works** of God. She holds the mysteries, the hidden wisdom of God (one perfect man of many). The new men of one heart will be made up of the infinite characteristics of both king and priest after the order of Christ. This unified heart is framed in the heavens and stored up in the holy city of God. Within the eternal, **wisdom** was there to witness what all that God had done and when God placed the *world* (Olam, the eternal) in the hearts of kings; in this wise, **wisdom** had become their counselor (all taking counsel together). The eternal vision of God proceeds from wisdom eyes and his blueprints are engraved on the hearts of kingdom leaders for the perfecting of his kings.

The most beautiful aspect of kingdom leadership is that at a *timeless point* in the heart, these prophetic blueprints take on a lifelike, realistic quality of perfection in the present **now**. These brief moments of the eternal produces momentous anticipation for the prophetic blueprints to become applicable and accomplished. It is at these *timeless points* that once the intuitive interpretation of **unity** has been internalized, then kingdom leaders can freely enact their relationship to eternity. In other words, God's time even "**now**" is omnipresent and is where **wisdom** lives. This is the "**now**" dimension of **wisdom**, that true kingdom leaders must be able to visualize the tangible representation of this higher dimension in order to grasp the full meaning of the *"**Revelation of Christ**"*. Those who accept the fact that God's **time** is perfect and complete in and of itself will bring regeneration within their perfecting process. This means that the actual accomplishment of God's purpose will bring the end in view. Attainment of the destined **work** will be perfectly accomplished; whereby, the prophetic promises are fulfilled and the beginning of a greater attainment is made possible. <u>This is the *extirpating work* of perfected **kings**. These are those kingdom leaders that have overcome the opposition of the world debt systems though Gods will and plan for our lives.</u>

You are probably asking yourself, "How does the *landscape* look"? How do you measure the **holy city** of God (the four square city) which is intangible? The measurement of the holy city is immeasurable and the standard is of Christ who is infinite. His *landscape* is divine and its inhabitants understand their heavenly presents as heavenly citizens who are immensely *unified* in the world. Another *critical element* to understand about the kingdom of God is to spiritually understand the *landscape* of the holy city, the intangible foundation made up of the walls and gates.

In addition, to seeing our own perfection, (complete wholeness, totality, and entireness) we as kingdom leaders must also be able to perceive and seize the mental picture of our qualitatively new *landscape* more than the old quantitatively. The *landscape* of the kingdom of God (The New Jerusalem) is present and *unified* within the minds, hearts, and souls of perfected kings; therefore, bringing forth the revelation of Christ. Making us conscious of our new and regenerated *landscape* that's within us and again, you are probably asking yourself, "how do you measure the New Jerusalem, the **holy city** of God, the four square city?" The measurement of the **holy city** and the New Jerusalem is immeasurable and the standard is of Christ who is infinite. "How does this *landscape* look"? The perfect work of matured men measured after the stature of Christ, the fullness of the Godhead actually manifested as one new man **unified** as one heart. This is how the future *landscape* will look which is lived divinely and its inhabitants are the heavenly citizens who will be immensely *unified* in the world. **The faith work of the kingdom isn't based on what God has done in time past but what we must do within ourselves to bring the future (aeons) into our present.** This beautiful metaphoric vision in Revelation 21: 9-27 is implied by the Messianic foundations according to its garnished walls is a resemblance of what have been literally manifested then as the *unified* man; although now, it is rarely understood how to actually apply it literally today.

As a result, our literal interpretation is disconnected from the implied promises of God and therefore, limited to receive the phenomenon through what the figurative represents; instead of receiving the inevitable and demonstrative surprise that we should expect from a good prophetic hypothetical metaphor. Never the less, the connection should be made between the implied comparisons of this metaphor and its comprehensive unity of the twelve tribes. Until this is done, the integrity of the interrelationships will always be divided.

The DNA of the Bride of Christ: Unity and Resurrection

Is. 9:6 <u>For to us a Child is born, to us a Son is given;</u>

Rev. 1:8 <u>I am Alpha and Omega, the first and the last [the beginning and the ending], said the Lord, **which is**, and **which was**, and **which is to come**, the Almighty.</u>

Eph. 3:10 *<u>[The purpose is] that through the church the complicated, many-sided wisdom of God in all its infinite variety and innumerable aspects might now be made known to the angelic rulers and authorities (principalities and powers) in the heavenly sphere.</u>*

Eph. 4:*24 and put on the new nature (the regenerate self) created in God's image, [Godlike] in true righteousness and holiness.*

Mt. 19:28 *<u>And Jesus said unto them, Verily I say unto you, that ye which have followed me, in the regeneration when the Son of Man shall sit in the throne of His glory, ye also shall sit upon twelve thrones, judging the twelve tribes of Israel</u>.*

Eph. 1:10 *<u>He planned for the maturity of the times and the climax of the ages to unify all things and head them up and consummate them in Christ, [both] things in heaven and things on the earth</u>.*

Jn. 17:1, 4, 5, 10, 11, 13, 15, 18, 20-24; *1)* When Jesus had spoken these things, He lifted up His eyes to heaven and said, Father, **the hour has come**. Glorify and exalt and honor and magnify Your Son, so that Your Son may glorify and extol and honor and magnify You. *4)* I have **glorified** You down here on the earth by completing the work that You gave Me to do.

5) And now, Father glorify Me along with Yourself and restore Me to such majesty and honor in Your presence as I had with You before the world existed. *10) All mine are Yours, and Yours are mine; and I am glorified in them. 11)* And [now] I am no more in the world, but these are [still] in the world, and I am coming to you. Holy Father, keep in Your name *those whom You have given Me, that they may be one as We are one. 13)* And **now** I am coming to You; I say these things while I am still in the world, so that My joy may be made full and complete and perfect in them, [that they may experience My delight fulfilled in them, that My enjoyment may be perfected in their own souls, that they may have My gladness within them, filling their hearts]. *15)* I do not ask that You will take them out of the world, but that You will keep and protect them from the evil one. *18)* Just as You **sent** Me into the world, I also have **sent** them into the world. *20)* Neither for these alone do I pray, but also for all those who will ever

24

come to believe in (trust in, cling to, rely on) Me through their word and teaching. *21) That they all may be one, [just] as You, Father, are in Me and I in You, that they also may be one in Us, so that the world may believe and be convinced that You have* **sent** *Me. 22)* I have given to them the glory and honor which You have given to Me, that they may be one [even] as We are one. *23) I in them and You in Me, in order that they may become one and perfectly united*, that the world may know and [definitely] recognize that You **sent** Me and that You have **loved them** [even] as You have **loved Me.** *24)* Father, I will that they also, who You have given Me, be with me where I am; that they may behold My glory, which You have given Me: for You loved Me before the foundation of the world.

Rev 1:6 *And hath made us **kings and priests** unto God and His Father; to Him be glory and dominion for ever and ever.*

Lk 22:29, 30 *I appointed unto you a kingdom, as My Father hath appointed unto me: 30) That ye may eat and drink at My table in My kingdom, and sit on thrones judging the twelve tribes of Israel.*

Col 2:2-3 [For my concern is] that their hearts may be braced (comforted, cheered, and encouraged) as they are **knit together** in love, that they may come to have all the abounding wealth and blessings of assured conviction of understanding, and, [which is Christ the anointed One]. *3) In Him all the treasures of [divine] wisdom comprehensive insight into the ways and purposes of God and [all the riches of spiritual] knowledge and enlightened are stored up and lie hidden.*

Jn 4:35 Do you not say, It is still four months until harvest time comes? Look! I tell you, raise your eyes and observe the fields and see how they are **already** white for harvesting.

1 Cor. 3: 9, 10; 9) For we are fellow workmen (joint promoters, laborers together) with and for God; you are God's garden and vineyard and **field** under cultivation, [you are] God's building. *10)* According to the grace (the special endowment for my task) of God bestowed on me, like a skillful architect and master builder I laid the foundation, and now another man is building upon it. But let each [man] be careful how he builds upon it. Eph 2:21 *In Him the whole structure is joined (bound, welded) together harmoniously, and it continues to rise (grow, increase) into a holy temple in the Lord [a sanctuary dedicated, consecrated, and sacred to the presence of the Lord].*

1 Cor 3:11 For no other foundation can anyone lay than that which is [already] laid which is Christ Jesus the [Anointed One].

1 Cor 3:16 Do you not discern and understand that you [the whole church of Corinth] are God's temple (His sanctuary), and that God's Spirit has His permanent dwelling in you [to be at home in you collectively as a church and also individually]?

Eph 2:6 And He raise us up together with Him and made us sit down together [giving us joint seating with Him] in the heavenly sphere;] by virtue of our being in Christ Jesus or the Messiah, or the Anointed One].

Eph 2:20-22; 20) and are built upon the foundations of the apostles and prophets, Jesus Christ Himself being the chief cornerstone; 21) In whom all the building fitly framed together grew into a holy temple in the Lord; Ref. Heb 11:40 22) In whom you also are built together for a habitation of God through the Spirit.

Eph 3:17, 18 That Christ may dwell in your hearts by faith; that ye being rooted and grounded in love, *18)* May be able to comprehend with all saints what is the breadth, and length, and depth, and height;

Eph 4:2-6; *2)*Living as becomes you with complete lowliness of mind (humility) and meekness (unselfishness, gentleness, mildness) with patience, bearing with one another and making allowances because you **love** one another. *3)* Be eager and strive earnestly to guard and keep the harmony and **oneness** of [and produced by] the Spirit in the binding power of peace. 4) There is one body and one Spirit - just as there is also one hope [that belongs] to the calling you received. 5) There is one Lord, one faith, one baptism, 6) One God and Father of [us] all, Who is above all [Sovereign over all], pervading all and [living] in [us] all.

1 Cor 15:27, 28) For He [the Father] has put all things in subjection under Christ's feet. But when it says, all things are put in subjection [under Him], it is evident that He [Himself] is expected Who does the subjecting of all things to Him. 28) However, when everything is subjected to Him, then the Son Himself will also subject Himself to [the Father] Who put all things under Him, so that God may be all in all. [Be everything to everyone, supreme, the indwelling and controlling factor of life]!

Eph 4:13 [That it might develop] until we all attain oneness in the faith and in the comprehension of the [full and accurate] knowledge of the Son of God, that [we might arrive] at really mature manhood (the completeness of personality which is nothing less than the standard height of Christ's own perfection), the measure of stature of the fullness of the Christ and the completeness found in Him.

Eph. 4:16 For because of Him the whole body (the church, in all its various parts), closely joined and firmly knit together by the joints and ligaments with which it is supplied, when each part [with power adapted to its need] is working properly [in all its functions], grows to full maturity, building itself up in love.

2 Cor. 5:1 For we know that if the tent which is our body earthly home is destroyed (dissolved), we have from God a building, a house not made with hands, eternal in the heavens.

Mk. 14:5 I will destroy this temple made with hands, and within three days I will build another made without hands.

Eph. 6:11 Put on God's whole armor [the armor of a heavy-armed soldier which God supplies], that you may be able successfully to stand up against [all] the strategies and the deceits of the devil. Eph. 6:14-17 Stand therefore [hold your ground], having tightened the **belt of truth** around your loins and having put on the breastplate of integrity and of moral rectitude and right standing with God, **15)** And having shod your **feet in preparation** [to face the enemy with the firm-footed stability, the promptness, and the readiness produced by the good news] of the Gospel of peace. **16)** Lift up over all the [covering] **shield** of saving faith, upon which you can quench all the flaming missiles of the wicked [one]. **17)** And take the **helmet** of salvation and the **sword** that the spirit wields, which is the Word of God.

Mk. 13:1, 2 And Jesus was coming out of the temple [area] one of His disciples said to Him. Look, Teacher! Notice the sort and quality of these stones and buildings! *2)* And Jesus replied to him, you see these great buildings? There will not be left here one stone upon another that will not be loosened and torn down.

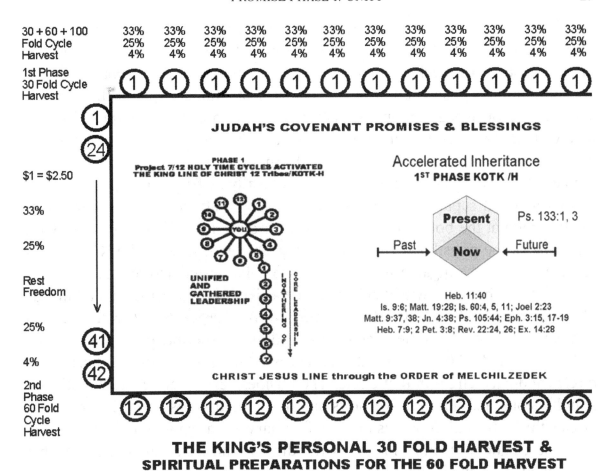

Figure 4

FIGURE 4 GRAPH EXPLANATION

Figures 4 and 7 associated profitability indicated the progressive ascension of God's various harvest feasts of old which is translated today as blessings and resembles the business cycles coming forth from God's kingdom across all 12 circles through all 3 levels. The activity of *figure 4* reveals the manifestation of the perfect will of the Most High God through his mysteries and allowing the leadership of God to align more closely to the business structures of kingdom economics. Finally, the beginning process of submission by the Aaronic priesthood or traditional church should conclude with the transition into the office of the kingship to increase and become magnified for the glory of Christ through the success of the leadership of the body of Christ. Project 7/12 is the ordained structure or business model on earth that God uses to bless his leadership and the promise seed who claim their inheritance in order for some to bring forth 30, 60, 100 fold harvests

The 4 graphics in *figure 3* start and finish at project 27/ phase 4 and moves clockwise to project 7/12-phase 1 then to project 4/phase 3 and its structural diagram and return back again to project 27/phase 4. Project 27/phase 4 is the consummation of phase 1 and phase 3. The project number explains the spiritual significance of that graph and activity necessary to achieve the promise and receive true blessings and inheritance from God. For example; the number 8 means resurrection or new beginnings and although, in *figures 2 and 5* of project 8/phase 2 the priesthood is represented graphically as fragmented, divided and denominational separatism and is illustrated by flattened circles (narrow at the top wide at the bottom) with a downward direction, it is the grace of God that renews the priesthood financially when the structures of the KOTK-H is resurrected and the ingathering of the KOTG is harvested and restored.

In *figure 4* the reader will be able to relate the likeness between the simultaneous blessings of the (30, 60, 100) fold harvests of old across the 12 tribes, and its simulation of the holy time cycles presented as **compound percentages** (4%, 25%, 33%, and 10,000% payout etc.) across the whole of the 12 horizontal circles and each circle in that circle. The business cycles are characteristically simultaneous and accelerative blessings distributed across the 12 horizontal circles throughout all 3 phases (the 3-3 fold harvests as shown in *figures 4 and 7*) of the kingdom organization for extraordinary manifestation of blessings that are reaped as shown in *figure 9*.

Project 7/12 is the ordained structure or business model on earth that God uses to bless his leadership and the promise seed who claim their inheritance in order for some to bring forth 30, 60,100 fold harvests and be blessed as a result of it. Faith and hope is represented by the mustard seeds and is the greatest factor in magnifying the operations and predestined works of the spirit bringing blessings to the leaders of God rapidly.

The Kingdom of the Kings and Heirs:
Predestination of Sonship
2nd Phase: 60 Fold Cycle Harvest

Mt. 13:17 Truly I tell you many prophets and righteous men [men who were upright and in right standing with God], yearned to see what you see, and did not see it, and to hear, and did not hear it.

Is. 9:6 For unto us a child is born, unto us a son is given:

1 Pe. 1:23 *You have been regenerated [born from above], not from a mortal, corruptible seed, but from one that is immortal, incorruptible, by the ever living and lasting word of God.* Lk. 22:29 *And as My Father has appointed a kingdom and conferred it on Me, so I do confer on you [the privilege and decree].* **Mt. 19:28** *And Jesus said unto them, verily I say unto you that ye which have followed Me, in the regeneration when the Son of man shall sit in the throne of His glory, ye also shall sit upon twelve (12) thrones, judging the twelve (12) tribes of Israel.* **Mt 19:29** *anyone and everyone who has left houses or brothers or sisters or father or mother or children or lands for My name's sake will receive many [even a hundred] times more and will inherit eternal life.*

Zech. 6:13 ***Yes, [you are building a temple of the Lord, But] it is He who shall build the [true] temple of the Lord, and He shall bear the honor and glory [as of the only begotten of the Father] and shall sit and rule upon His throne and He shall be a Priest upon His throne, and the counsel of peace shall be between the two [offices - Priest and king].*** *Rev. 1:6 And formed us into a kingdom [a royal race], priests to His God and Father - to Him be the glory and the power and the majesty and the dominion throughout the ages and forever and ever.* Amen [so be it]**.**

John 4: 35) Say ye not, there are yet four (4) months and then cometh the harvest? Behold, I say unto you, lift up your eyes, and look on the fields. For the fields are already white for harvest.

Gen. 22:17 ***In blessing I will bless you and in multiplying I will multiply your descendants like the stars of the heavens and like the sand on the seashore. And your seed [heir] will possess the gate of his enemies.***

1Pe. 2:5 *[Come] and, like living stones, be yourselves built [into] a spiritual house, for a holy (dedicated, consecrated) priesthood, to offer up [those] spiritual sacrifices [that are] acceptable and pleasing to God through Jesus Christ.*

Mal. 3:4 Then the offering of Judah and Jerusalem will be pleasant to the Lord, as in days of old, as in the former years. Joel 2:23 Be glad then, you children of Zion, and rejoice in the Lord, your God; for He gives you the former or early rain in just measure and in righteousness, and he causes to come down for you the rain, the former rain and the latter rain in the [1st] first month. 36) And he that reaped received wages [he who does the cutting now has his reward], for he is gathering fruit unto life eternal, so that he who does the planting or sowing and he who does the reaping may rejoice together.

John 4:38 *I sent you to reap a crop for which you have not toiled. Other men have labored and you have stepped in to reap the results of their work.* Ref Dut 6:10, 11

Mt. 9:38 Pray ye therefore the Lord of the Harvest, that He will send forth laborers into His harvest. Is 60:3, 4; **And nations shall come to your light, and kings to the brightness of your rising. Lift up your eyes round about you and see! They all gather themselves together, they come to you. Your sons shall come from afar. And your daughters shall be carried and nursed in the arms.**

Is. 60:5, 11; Then you shall see and be radiant, and your heart shall thrill and tremble with joy [at the glorious deliverance] and be enlarged; because the abundant wealth of the [Dead] Sea shall be turned to you, unto you shall the nations come with their treasuries. And your gates shall be open continually, they shall not be shut day and night, the men may bring to you the wealth of the nations - and their kings led in procession.

Ps. 133:1 Behold, how good and how pleasant it is for brethren to dwell together in **unity** [as the heart of one man, one heart.]Ps. 133:3) As the dew of Hermon, and as the dew that descended upon the mountains of Zion: For there the Lord commanded the blessing, even life for evermore.

NOTE: Zion. The dew (or abundant summer nite mist) was one. The same dew descended on Zion in the south as on Mount Hermon in the north. Zion's dew represents the tribe of Judah. Hermon's dew represents Asher, Ephraim, Manasseh, Zebulon, Issachar - The idea is not in the direction of this dew, from Hermon to Zion, **but in its uniting both in its copious descent.** Jn. 12:24 Most assuredly, I say to you, unless a grain of a mustard seed falls into the ground and dies, it remains alone; [it never becomes more but lives], But if it dies, it produces many others and yields a rich harvest. **Ex. 1:7 But the descendants of Israel were fruitful and increased abundantly; they multiplied and grew exceedingly strong; and the land was full of them. Dut. 7:9 Know, recognize, and understand therefore that the Lord your God, He is God. The faithful God, Who keeps covenant and steadfast love and mercy with those who love Him and keep His commandments, to a thousand generations. Num. 26:54-56; to the larger tribe you shall give the greater inheritance, and to a small tribe the less inheritance; to each tribe shall its inheritance be given according to its numbers. But the land shall be divided by lot; according to the names of the tribes of their fathers they shall inherit and their inheritance shall be divided between the larger and the smaller.**

Rev. 19:7, 8; 7) Let us be glad and rejoice, [exulting and triumphant]! Let us celebrate and ascribe to Him glory and honor, for the marriage of the Lamb [at last] has come, and His bride has prepared herself. 8) She has been permitted to dress in fine (radiant) linen, dazzling and white - for the fine linen is [signifies, represents] the righteousness [the upright, just, and Godly living, deeds, and conduct, and right standing with God] of the saints, God's holy people.

PROMISE PHASE 1: UNITY
INTERLUDE: The Overshadowing Lie

Matthew 13:30 Let both of them grow together until the harvest: and in the time of the harvest I will say to the reapers, gather together first the tares, and bind them in bundles to burn them: but gather the wheat into my barn.

The subordinate position of folly appears to have underscore wisdom and have moved to the forefront in the commonplace mindset of society today. Society has sanctimoniously legitimized the lie as reality against wisdom. This super symbolic paradigm has been justified with such intensity that man is acutely conscious of sharp inconsistencies everywhere but is chronically impervious to change it. Every attempt to reform the situation only piles on and makes the bad conditions worse. This plausible activity only propels the reformation into deeper levels of insanity, perplexity, and confusion while growing further away from the truth.

These complexities and their inherent contradictions in the world are so great that they can't be solved or represented adequately by just one aspect alone. Our irreversible struggle has always been and will continue to be that any possible choice between two evils will always lead to multiple evils. When exposing the lie the Truth alone is the only separator that brings both sorrow and inevitably joy during the purging process. It is very difficult to get back on the right track when one believes that they are on the right track when in actuality they are on the wrong track. The result that brings no sorrow but peace will help determine rather you are on the right track. From every channel of media today society is bombarded daily with the pessimistic conditions of these complexities and contradictions.

That is why society from the top down has become disconnected from truth because our propositions which appear to be plausible are in fact, contradictory and mere demagogue. This dogmatic style of short term thinking permeates throughout the political, economic and religious arena. The results are retrograded and its consequences trickle down even to the unborn. This only leads to continuous disputes because long term dilemmas can not be solved by short term answers. As a result, the repeated backwardness carried over long periods of time only intensify the conditions making the consequences even worse; thereby, shielding the light or solutions from view. The truth behind the contradictions and hypocrisy in most of our misunderstandings aren't consistent with what we think reality in our lives is and the events surrounding us should be; therefore, the truth isn't immediately apparent to us, and as a result our expectations will not be met if we continue depending on these misunderstandings. What we think is right is actually wrong and the wrong is thought to be right and that is why the paradoxical statement of Shakespeare in that "there is nothing good or bad (right or wrong), but thinking makes it so" have a great deal of ambiguity when first read. The accepted fact of what must be must be sounds preposterous. But it is this very lack of not seeing both sides instead of just that one side is the absurdity that humor reveals in our own lives. Here lies the essence of most **paradoxical events** utilized by Christ which was to reveal the connections between apparent opposites and combining both actualities which have a connecting point of a deeper reality and a later truth.

Therefore, the **hypothetical** metaphors were the backdrop for which Christ used to target his enemies characteristic inconsistencies was the self righteousness among the religious community primarily the Sanhedrin council. Their righteous pretensions and especially the Pharisaic spirit became the battlefield was Christ major weapon of humor and laughter, which he used fully against the fierce enmity of the religious opposition. Even in most of our experiences today, our understanding tends to run parallel along these same lines as Christ enemies who could not see the Truth behind the humor; consequently, their one sided assumptions have always been conflicting and looked upon Jesus with disdain and rejection.

This persistent behavior of stupidity was illustrated by Christ's most intractable enemies the Pharisee, which included the Sadducees; as well as the priest and scribes, which Christ considered to be the least of them all. The irony of Christ humor seemed to have been hostile, harmful, and even sarcastic toward religion; but in actuality it wasn't. Christ caused attention though his penetrating Truth and exposed with shocking insight the inconceivable absurdities of the spirit of Satan. Unfortunately, because of the absurdity was held up in public view with no attempt to harm He eventually became despised, hated and murdered.

Jesus profound wisdom always presented the beneficial hypotheses that only he could have provided. Solutions that would otherwise remain unsolved now call attention to the promises that Jesus exemplified against the self contradicting paradox to call attention to hypothesis that would, otherwise without it, remain hidden. The self discovery of Jesus arsenal will always reveal various aspects of the truth. It is this great appreciation for Jesus works that bring forth a delightful surprise; and eventually, a sense of relief when perplexing dilemmas are clarified and understanding increased. The strategy of Christ laughter and the irony used from his arsenal was utilized in his metaphors to attack those who were self deluded. This is the consequential effects of being overwhelmingly ignorant eventually leading to self exclusion.

Elton Trueblood in his book 'The Humor of Christ' realized a central feature in laughter that being, "humor is always a concealed pair." For example, in Mt.3:9; Jn.8:37, 39 when Jesus told the Pharisees and the Sadducees not to think Abraham was there father although he recognized that they were from Abraham seed (at least sown into it), but the spirit behind their work was not of Abraham seed but the Devil, the liar and murderer.

When kingdom leaders lay the axe at the roots of this **dichotomy**; between where the truth begins and the lie ends; then as kingdom leaders we can distinguish with simplicity what is often exceedingly hard to identify. Here is where Satan's lie is exposed within his **duplicity** the chaotic dispersion of his substratum, subdivisions and its stratagem from time past to present. The humor of Christ can now be seen and extracted from the complexities of Satan's flood of lies. Christ laid open for us the understanding needed to overcome this **sublime dualism**: the priesthood of Moses and Aaron and the priesthood of the Sanhedrin sect are two separate institutions interwoven as one which must be understood that both are not of Christ lineage but that of Satan seed transformed! Unfortunately, the majority of church leadership today has progressively existed between these two antiquated extremes; while at the same time, reluctantly moving more towards the secular and political power of the surrounding paganism which is inherent to this type of **juxtapose**. Although the sources may be ancient the roots of its operation are perpetually transposed in these modern times. While the metamorphosis is rarely discerned, its economic snare of the accepted world debt system is intangibly present and the **evanescent schism** associated with any **hybrid**.

To reiterate at this point **Lucifer** who became his own god **"is the god of this world" but is now Satan, who follows his own spirit which is "the spirit of the world" is to no avail is trying to build his own divided kingdom which is "the kingdom of this world"** and that exist out side of Christ kingdom. This is Satan's modus operandi or method of operation to kill, steal and destroy all while remaining hidden. That is why Christ in [Rev.2:9; 3:9] admonishes kingdom leaders to be aware of those who claim to be of our brother Judah/Christ but is not. We are to beware [and keep] away from, or clear of the "**leaven**" or their teachings and to understand the operations of the "*synagogue of Satan*" and its evil effects his kingdom has upon his own world monetary, economic, and investment systems of today and how it has become the accepted way of life. This is Satan's sphere of activity to oppose God's Word and create resistance to its Truth.

But unfortunately today, the blind leadership of the mega churches has become too secularized within their own theology to teach the accurate and perfect Word of Truth producing immature teaching and consequently, babes in Christ. They actually need to be taught again because the economic pressures of the world debt system has forced the church leadership to focus their message more toward prosperity, tithes and offerings, which have taken center stage and is the prevalent activity (working harder on the job for less) for the church members. The teaching of prosperity is to no avail unfortunately, because it is predicated on the world debt system. Outside of that the religious teaching is impractical in implementing God divine plan and purpose for accomplishing these objectives. Although the church tithes are generated from the debt system kingdom leaders should provide the kingdom wealth that true tithes and offerings should come from and not the debt system.

The proper application of kingdom principles produces **wealth** and prosperity which includes tithes and offerings which are by products of kingdom economics. **Wealth** must first come though the proper kingdom structure, then prosperity will flow over into not just the church but the whole family of God as a natural extension to his kingdom on earth. Therefore by default, the church leadership of today themselves has become some what like the Sadducees the **privileged priestly** families of Jerusalem still dependent on the contributions of their congregations who in turn are dependent on their jobs which are tied to the debt system. But if the jobs aren't there or the congregants are laid off due to the ill health of the world economic system then the church struggles and must become politically dependent and shrewd within the walls of pagan economic captivity.

Compromising with the existing political order and economic dependency on the world system have created as a result, the worldliness of its congregations and the torpid state of mind and spiritual depravity which prevents one from seeing or receiving the truth of the present economy of the kingdom. I know this is hard for the self righteous to grasp, but, if the traditional minded Christians can actually see themselves to some extent as Pharisees who Christ targeted the most among the three sects, then the valuable wit and laughter of Christ could become a valuable redemptive process of purification from the bondage of the lie and self exclusion from the kingdom of God and the desperate inclusion into the world debt system.

The implied parable in Mt.13: 24-30 of the **wheat and tares** shows the radical metaphor that Christ used to identify the tares as the serpent seed of Satan. I often wondered why not separate the wheat from the tares. Because as a young boy I have pulled up weeds just to have them grow back stronger not understanding the agricultural process. The tares are almost the same in color and therefore indistinguishable from wheat and until they are full grown the tares are long, black and bitterly poisonous. But after the maturation process each grain must be removed first before grinding the wheat. Christ showed us the answer by loving his enemies and being diligent about doing his fathers will and finishing his fathers business and not entangled in Satan's business.

The truth of the matter is that he probably would have gone to the cross much sooner had not the people asked for healings and overcoming the sins of the world with authority by performing prophetic miracles. These distractions were of course manifested for us to benefit from today though Jesus example. This is a tough pill to swallow until we realize that God and Christ can not lie "that all these things must come to pass". In other words, Satan's plan must run its course. And any attempt to prohibit Satan's plan is like fighting God too! Secondly, but equally as important, Christ reveals the antidote to life application against the evil affects of **Satan divide**. The enemy the devil who planted his seeds is allowed to grow up with the wheat instead of being separated from it. In other words; as kingdom leaders, don't try to mend the divide. That is like trying to patch up a dam after the hole have ruptured and water is pouring out as if the flood gates were opened.

The **church leadership** then (the Scribes, Pharisees and the Sadducees) has always condemned Jesus for all the good that he shown and all the miracles he performed for the masses. Everything he done always went against their traditions and the culture of the world. We need to understand why Jesus identified them as not being from **Abraham seed** but of the serpent seed. Their father the devil (as the murderer and the liar) who being the father of the lie since the beginning and the evil works that their fathers have done before them they will and must do also. Here, the same model set forth then is today greatly changed into many different forms of religious denominations and non-religious organization over the course of a long and changing history. Unfortunately, the cause and operation of Satan is still the same to kill, steal, and destroy. It is ironic that Satan main focus was and still is though the fragmented religious organizations and their denominations as well as the political system that are divided.

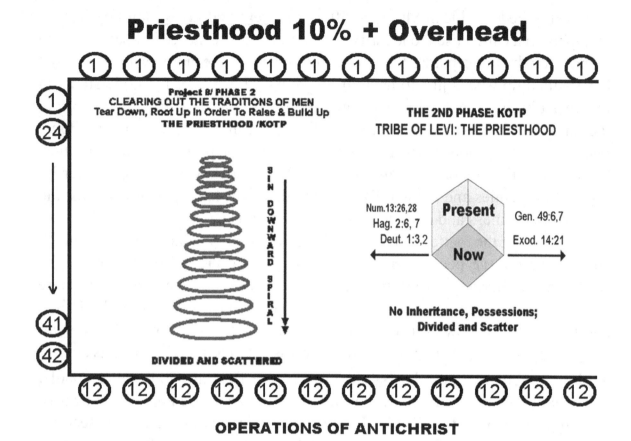

Figure 5

FIGURE 5 GRAPH EXPLANATION

There are 5 diagrams in *figures 4, 5, 6, 7, and 9* that have horizontal lines with circles attached representing the souls of man. In *figures 4 and 7* the rectangle box shows the separation of the king/priest office. It also is the closed condition of the priest office when the transition from priest to king haven't occurred and the resources are limited to the 10% tithe, instead of the kingdom offering. king office: (the horizontal line 12 circles with the # 12 in them for the 12 tribes) and the priest office (12 circles with the # 1 in them) represents the general traditional church stemming from the levitical priesthood which are scattered throughout all 12 tribes and submitting to the king's office illustrated by the other open diagrams in *figures 3 and 9.*

The graphs in *figures 2, 5, and 7* which represents the church, has infinite potential only if it integrates into promise phases 1 of *figures 3 and 6* Only from a practical stand point, when these 2 entities, the church and the kingship, are integrated into the two kingdom principles of kingdom economics and kingdom leadership. Then, will the two offices of the priesthood and the kingship be galvanized into a larger class of unified leadership and into higher dimensions of the kingdom wealth. Creating an implosion within the new leadership structures and a ubiquitous influx of redistributed wealth.

Since the Financial pie of the world's debt system is forever shrinking, the church must produce other forms of income streams outside of the 10% tithe, because the majority of those who produce the tithe for the church are dependent on the worlds' debt system, job and investment markets that is having an extremely negative impact on how they produce their profit potential and income generation. In order for the church to increase their 10% to 10,000% to 10,000,000% they would have to transition practically into the larger aspects and levels of the kingdom. In other words, by the priesthood transposing their position spiritually with the practical physical (not abstract) position of their kingship the profit motive of the church can be removed. When the church transition from *figures 2 & 5* into the king line of Judah/Christ seen in *figures 4, 6, 7 and 9;* then, the gaps between the 4 circles suddenly closes vertically, producing simultaneously wealth redistributing over all circles within circle 42. The proleptic aspect of the prophetic blueprint of Christ is rarely understood when it comes to manifesting our past or future promises and blessings in our present now today, but, that's why when this particular aspect is understood by the heirs (multiplicity of spiritual kings) of Christ then we can become overcomers in the invisible economy of the marketplace.

Ascending wealth will be distributed simultaneously across 1000's of generations; with its reciprocal facets of kingdom wealth exclusively expanded between circle 41 (the operations of Christ's spirit) and circle 42 (the multiplicity of Christ's spiritual kings) this is the 2n1 phenomenon in Christ ref. pages 18, which extends both vertically and horizontally. The vertical integration of circle 1 [is actually the 12 circles of 1's (illustrating all the consummated and economic activity horizontally within circle 1 as being the heritage of Jacob) ref. pages 28, 37, 66 to 68 and 130; *figures 4 and 7]*; again, with circle 1 and circle 24 integrating together into circle 41 as one within circle 41 (the kingdom leadership structure of Christ). Here are the points of transitions where kingdom wealth is horizontally magnified and disbursed throughout circle 42 encompassing all 12 circles: [of 1's(12) all the 12 circles of 12's(144) and all the 12 circles of 10k(10,000,s) or 12 times 10,000's; while further being superimposed ubiquitously upon the multiplicity of spiritual kingships and beyond to their kingdom structures, as indicated in *figures 4 and 9*, ref. pages 130 to 133. Now the church and its 10% tithe immediately becomes infused with phase 1 wealth implosion of the 30 fold king's harvest, in addition to the compound influx of the 60 fold leadership harvest all while being magnified by phase 3 and its 100 fold harvests (10,000%) of the nation and its generations of today represented as the same circle, both as circle 42 or the 42nd generation all in circle 1. This Ref. page 130 and 133, and *figure 9*.

Wealth is distributed 12 circles of 1's (all the consummated activity within circle 1 as circle 24 being the church), and all 12 circles of 12(144) and all 12 circles of 10k(10,000), throughout the 12(10k) circles or 12 times 10,000 which is 120,000 circles as indicated in *figure 9*. Now the church and its 10% tithe immediately becomes infused with phase 1 wealth implosion of the 30 fold king's harvest, in addition to the compound influx of the 60 fold leadership harvest all while being magnified by phase 3 and its 100 fold harvests (10,000%) of the nation and its generations of today represented as the same circle, both as circle 42 or the 42nd generation all in circle 1.

The unification and gathering in of the core leadership of phase 1 of this figure is the only way to offset the downward sin cycles of debt in phase 2 of *figures 2 and 5*. When the church transition from *figures 2 and 5*, (the 10% tithe) to *figures 3, 6, and 9* (combined with the 30, 60, and 100 fold or 10,000% harvest of *figures 4 and 7*) then all the gaps between the king's office and the office of the priest will quickly close and both offices will be glorified exponentially as a result of bringing forth our royal heritage of Jacob/Christ and ushering in the extraordinary and ubiquitous phenomenon of the DNA of Christ. Reference page 44 "Church solution" of the book.

It is at this point, the reader must remember that the other figures regardless of their variations stems from *figure 1* and is the paramount figure representing the present now dimensions. **Figures 4 and 7 associated profitability indicated the progressive ascension of God's various harvest feasts of old which is translated today as blessings and resembles the business cycles coming forth from God's kingdom across all 12 circles through all 3 levels. The activity of *figure 4* reveals the manifestation of the perfect will of the Most High God through this revelatory knowledge of the mystery of the church for the unique leadership of God to align more closely to the business model of kingdom economics. Finally, the beginning process of submission by the Aaronic priesthood or the traditional church must conclude with the transitional shift into the other of the two offices. Namely, that the covenant blessings of Judah will be increased, along with the office of the kingship becoming magnified; in order for the** succession of Christ's glory can pass through all the body of Christ and its foundations rise like the sun.

The Kingdom of the Priests: (KOTP)
Self Examination and Sin Identified

Gen 49: 5, 7; Simeon and Levi are brothers; instruments of cruelty are in their habitations. 7) Curse be their anger for it was fierce: and their wrath for it was cruel: I will divide them in Jacob and scatter them in Israel. Num 18: 20 And the Lord spoke to Aaron. You shall have no inheritance in their land, neither shall you have any part among them: I am your part and inheritance among the children of Israel. Joshua 19:1 And the second lot came forth to Simeon, even for the tribe of the children of Simeon according to their families: and their inheritance was within the inheritance of the children of Judah. [Ref. 2Cor 10: 15]

1 Jn 3:8, 9; 8) But he who commits sin [who practices evildoing] is of the devil]takes his character from the evil one], for the devil has sinned [violated the divine law from the beginning. The reason the Son of God was made manifest (visible) was to undo [destroy, loosen, and dissolve] the **works** the devil has done. **9)** No one born of God [deliberately, knowingly and habitually] practices sin, for God's nature abides in him [**His principled life, the divine sperm, remains permanently within him**]; and he can't practice sinning because he is born (begotten of God).

1 Jn 1:8 If we say we have no sin [refusing to admit that we are sinners], we delude and lead ourselves astray, and the truth does not dwell in our hearts.

1 Jn 1:10 If we claim we haven't sinned, we contradict His Word and make Him out to be false and a liar, and His Word is not in us.

Heb 4:11 Let us therefore be zealous and exert ourselves and strive diligently to enter that **rest** [of God, **to know and experience it for ourselves**], that no one may fall or perish by the same kind of **unbelief and disobedience** [as those in the wilderness fell]. **Heb 4:10** For he who has once entered God's rest also has ceased from [the weariness and pain] of human labors. Just as God rested from those labors peculiarly his own. Heb 4:9 So then, is still awaiting a full and complete Sabbath – rest reserved for the true people of God.

Heb 4:7 Again He sets a definite day, [a new] today, and gives another opportunity of securing that rest] saying through David after so long a time in the words already quoted, today, if you would hear His voice and when you hear it, do not harden your hearts.

Heb 4:6 *Seeing that the promise remains over [from past times] for some to enter that rest, and that those who formerly were given the good news about it and the opportunity, failed to appropriate it and did not enter because of disobedience.* Heb 4:2 For indeed <u>we have had the</u> Gospel of God proclaimed to us just as truly as **they** [the Israelites of old did when the good news of deliverance from bondage came to them]; but the message they heard did not benefit them], **because it was not mixed with faith** [with the leaning of the entire personality on God in absolute trust and confidence in His power, wisdom, and goodness] *by those who heard it; neither were they united in faith with the ones [Joshua & Caleb] who heard (did believe).*

Heb 4:1 Therefore, while the promise of entering His rest still holds and is offered [today], let us be afraid [to distrust it]. Lest any of you should think he has come too late and has come short of [reaching] it.

2 Cor 3:17 <u>Now the Lord is the Spirit,</u> and **<u>where the Spirit of the Lord is, there is liberty</u>** [emancipation from bondage, freedom]. Ref. Isa 61:1, 2

2 Tim 4:2 Herald and preach the Word! Keep your sense of urgency [stand by, be at hand and ready], whether the opportunity seems favorable or unfavorable. Whether it is convenient or inconvenient, whether it is welcome or unwelcome, **you as preacher** of the Word are to **show people** in what way their lives are wrong.] and convince them, rebuking and correcting, warning and urging and encouraging them, being unflagging and inexhaustible in patience and teaching. 2 Tim 4:3 For the time is coming when people will not endure sound and wholesome instruction, but having ears itching [for something pleasing and gratifying], they will gather to themselves one teacher after another to a considerable number, chosen to satisfy their own liking and to foster the errors they hold.

2 Tim 3:7 They are forever inquiring and getting information, but are never able to arrive at a recognition and knowledge of the truth. 2 Tim 3:6 For among them are those who worm their way into homes and captivate silly and weak-natured and spiritually dwarfed **women** loaded down with sins, and easily swayed led away by various evil desires and seductive impulses. 2 Tim 3:5 For although they hold a **form of piety** (true religion), they deny and reject and are strangers to the power of it [their conduct belies the genuineness of their profession]. Avoid all such people [turn away from them]. 2 Tim 3:4 They will be treacherous, betrayers, rash, inflated with self-conceit. They will be lovers of sensual pleasures and vain amusements more than lovers of God. 2 Tim 3:3 They will be without natural affection, admitting to no truce or relentless, slanderers or false accusers, troublemakers, intemperate-loose in morals and conduct, uncontrolled and fierce, haters of good. 2 Tim 3:2 For people will be lovers of self and [utterly self-centered], lovers of money and aroused by an inordinate [greedy] desire for wealth, proud and arrogant and contemptuous boasters. They will be abusive, blasphemous, scoffing, disobedient to parents, ungrateful, unholy and profane. 2 Tim 3:1 But understand this, that in the last days set in perilous times of great stress and trouble [hard to deal with and hard to bear]. Heb 6:1 Therefore let us go on and get past the elementary stage in the teaching and doctrine of Christ (the Messiah), advancing steadily toward the completeness and perfection that belong to spiritual maturity. Let us not again be laying the foundation of repentance and abandonment of dead works or [dead formalism] and of the faith [by which you turned] to God. Heb 9:14-17; How much more surely shall the blood of Christ, Who by virtue of His eternal Spirit [His own preexistent divine personality] has offered Himself as an unblemished sacrifice to God, purify our conscience from dead works and lifeless observances, to serve the ever living God? 15) [Christ, the Messiah] is therefore the Negotiator and Mediator of an entirely new agreement or [testament, covenant], so that those who are called and offered it may receive the fulfillment of the promised everlasting inheritance – since a Death has taken place which rescues and delivers and redeems them from the transgressions committed under the [old] first agreement. 16) For where there is a last will testament involved, the death of the one who made it must be established. 17) For a will testament is valid and take effect only at death, since it has no force or legal power as long as the one who made it is alive.

Note! In fact under the Law almost everything is purified by means of blood, and without the shedding of blood there is neither release from sin and its guilt nor the remission of the due and merited punishment for sins.

Heb 9:23-25 By means, therefore, it was necessary for the earthly copies of the heavenly things to be purified, but the actual heavenly things themselves required far better and nobler sacrifices than these.

24) For Christ has not entered into a sanctuary made with human hands, only a copy and pattern and type of the true one, but [Christ has entered] into heaven itself, now to appear in the very pressure of God on our behalf. 25) Nor did He [enter into the heavenly sanctuary to offer Himself regularly again & again, as the high priest enters the Holy of Holies every year with blood not his own.

Rom 3:4 By no means Let God be found true and every human being is false and a liar, as it is written, that you may be justified and shown to be upright in what you say, and overcome when you are judge. Ps 51:4

1 Pe 2:5 [Come and like living stones, be yourself built into] a spiritual house, for a holy dedicated, consecrated priesthood to offer up [those] spiritual sacrifices

[that are acceptable and pleasing to God through Jesus Christ. 1 Pe 2:9 But you are a chosen race, a royal priesthood, a dedicated nation, [God's] own purchased, special people, that you may set forth the wonderful deeds and display the virtues and perfections of Him Who called you out of darkness into His marvelous light.

Warning to the Priesthood

Amos 5:18, 19; 18)But **woe** to you who desire the day of the Lord! For what good is the day of the Lord to you? It will be darkness not light. *19)* It would be as though a man fled from a lion and a bear met him, or as though he went into a house, leaned his hand on a wall and a serpent bit him.

Amos 8:11 I will send a famine in the land, not a famine of bread nor a thirst for water. **But of hearing the words of the Lord**. 1 Cor. 4:18-21; 18) Some of you have become conceited and arrogant and pretentious, counting on my not coming to you. *19)* But I will come to you shortly, if the Lord is willing, and then I will perceive and understand not what the talk of these puffed up and arrogant spirits amount to, **but their force [the moral power and excellence of soul they really possess]**. *20)* **For the kingdom of God consists of and is based on not talk, but power** [moral power and excellence of soul]. *21)* Now which do you prefer? Shall I come to you with a rod of correction, and loving kindness.

Mt 19:30 But many who [now] are first will be last [then], and many who [now] are last will be first. Mt. 23:2-4, 11-12 The scribes and the Pharisees sit in Moses seat. *3)* Therefore whatever they tell you to observe that observe and do, **but do not do according to their works; for they say, and do not do**. *4)* For they bind heavy burdens, hard to bear, and lay them on men shoulders; but they themselves will not move them with one of their fingers. *11)* But he who is greatest among you shall be your servant. *12)* And he whoever exalts himself will be humbled, and he who humbles himself will be exalted. Lk 7:28 For I say to you, among those born of women there is not a greater prophet than John the Baptist; **but he who is least in the kingdom of God is greater than he**.

Mt. 23:13, 15-16 But **woe** to you, Scribes and Pharisees, hypocrites! For you shut up the kingdom of heaven against men; for you neither go in yourselves, nor do you allow those who are entering to go in. *15)* **Woe** unto you, Scribe and Pharisee, hypocrites! For ye compass sea and land to make one proselyte, and when he is made ye make him twofold more the child of hell than yourself. *16)* **Woe** to you blind guides, who say, if anyone swears by the sanctuary of the temple it is nothing; but if anyone swears by the gold of the sanctuary, **he is a debtor** [bound by his oath].

Mt. 23:28 **Woe** to you, Scribes and Pharisees, hypocrites! Even so you also outwardly appear righteous to men, but inside you are full of hypocrisy and lawlessness. Mt. 23:34, 37, 38; *34) Therefore, indeed I send you prophets, wise men, and scribes: some of them you will kill and crucify, and some of them you will scourge in your synagogues and persecute from city to city. 37) O Jerusalem, Jerusalem, the one who kills the prophets and stones those who are sent to her! How often I wanted to gather your children together, as a hen gathers her chicks under her wings, but you were not willing! 38)* See! Your house is forsaken and desolate [abandoned and left destitute of God's help].

Mk. 13:1, 2 <u>And as Jesus was coming out of the temple [area] one of His disciples said to Him, look, Teacher! Notice the sort and quality of these stones and buildings!</u> *2)* And Jesus replied to him, <u>you see these</u> great buildings? There will not be left here one stone upon another that will not be loosened and torn down.

Num. 14:31 But your little ones whom you said would be a prey. Them will I bring in and they shall know the land which you have despised and rejected. Hos. 4:1, 4-6 *1)* Hear the Word of the Lord, ye **children of Israel**: for the Lord hath a controversy with the inhabitants of the land, because there is no truth, not mercy, nor knowledge of God in the land. *4)* Yet let no man strive, nor reprove another: for thy people are as they that strive with the **priest**. *5)* Therefore shall thou fall in the day, and the **prophet** also shall fall with thee in the night, **and I will destroy thy mother** [the priestly nation]. *6)* My people are destroyed for lack of knowledge; because **you** [the priestly nations] <u>have rejected knowledge</u>, I will also reject you that you shall be no **priest** to Me; seeing you have forgotten the law of your God I will also forget your children.

Dut. 32:15 But **Jeshurun** grew fat and kicked; you grew fat, you grew thick, you are obese and scornfully esteemed the Rock of his salvation. Ps 106:32, 35-36; *32)* They angered Him also at the waters of strife, so that it went ill with Moses on account of them. *35)* But they mingled with the Gentiles and learned their works; *36)* They served their idols which became a snare to them. Num 16:13, 14 It is a small thing that you have brought us up out of a land flowing with milk and honey, to kill us in the wilderness, that you should keep acting like a prince over us? *14)* Moreover you have not brought us into a land flowing with milk and honey; nor given us inheritance of fields and vineyards. Will you put out the eyes of these men? We will not come up!

Ps. 106:37, 39, 41-42; *37)* They even sacrificed their sons and their daughters to demons. *39)* Thus they were defiled by their own works, and played the harlot by their own deeds. *41)* So that He abhorred His own inheritance. And He gave them into the hand of the Gentiles. *42)* Their enemies oppressed them, and they were bought into subject under their hand.

Dut. 32:35 Vengeance is Mine, and recompense; their foot shall slip in due time; for the day of their calamity is at hand. And the things to come hasten upon them. Phil. 3:7, 8 **But what things were gain to me, these I have counted loss for Christ**. *8)* I count all things as dung for the excellence of the knowledge of Christ Jesus my Lord for Whom I have suffered the loss of all things and count them as rubbish-dung to gain more of Christ.

Mal. 2:1-3 And now, O you **priest**, this commandment is for you. *2)* If you will not hear and if you will not lay it to heart to give glory to **My Name, the God of Jacob**, says the Lord of hosts, then I will send the **curse** upon you, and I will **curse** your blessings; yes, I have **already** turned them to **curses** because you don't lay it to heart.

3) Behold I will rebuke your seed [grain-which will prevent due harvest], and I will spread the dung from the festival offerings upon your faces, and you shall be taken away with it. Mal 2:17 You have wearied the Lord with your words. Yet you say, in what way have we wearied Him? [You do it when by your actions] you say. Everyone who does evil is good in the sight of the Lord and He delights in them. Or [by asking] where is the God of Justice. Mal 1:13 Ye also say, Behold, what a drudgery and weariness this is! And you have snuffed at it, said the Lord of hosts: and you brought that which was torn, and the lame, and the sick this you bring as an offering! Shall I accept this from your hand? Said the Lord.

Exod 18:14, 17-19, 21; *14)*When Moses father-in-law saw all that you do for the people he asked why do you sit alone, and all the people stand around you from morning till evening? *17)* Jethro said, **the time-consuming activity isn't good**. *18) You will surely wear away, both you and this people that are with you: **for this time consuming activity is too heavy for you:** you are not able to perform it by yourself alone*. *19)* Listen to my voice; I will give you counsel and God will be with you: Stand before God for the people, so that you may bring the difficulties to God. *21)* Moreover you shall select from all the peoples able men, such as fear the Lord, men of truth, hating covetousness; and place such over them to be rulers of thousands, rulers of hundreds, rulers of fifties, and rulers of tens.

Church Solution

But here lies the problem for the church leadership, they are trapped between the duality of religion and the dependency on political economics governance; but in addition to that, because **kingdom economics** isn't practically understood outside of both the predominate closed system of the church, and the prominent system of Satan's debt system and the church though the priesthood of Aaron even until today, as we unknowingly live and support these system daily primarily with debt capital, increase sin taxes, ineffective government programs, extended age for retiring and retirement benefits, longer hours on your jobs. So, as a result, the cultures of society are psychologically frustrated and financially burdened with the overwhelming conditions plaguing the systems in which we depend on for support is like quick sand. The more you struggle to get out the deeper you sink.

Therefore, the solution for society and the church specifically is that the principles of kingdom economics must extend beyond just preaching and teaching about it, but must be lived and practiced as a way of life and passed on from generation to generations. This requires a severe paradigm shift that extends well beyond the realm and perspective of our comfort zone we have within the world debt system. The key in establishing the practical secular framework and the structural models of **kingdom economics** must be founded in the word of God for the divine purpose of social and economic advancements. By default, however; until the **framework of kingdom economics** is implemented and utilized to this degree, by default, society as a whole, blacks and minorities in general and Christians specifically; consequently, the majority in society as it is will have no choice but depend more on the world debt system that is transposing and interposing itself upon the majority of the minority class; who are actually foreigners to the utilization of both the world economic monetary system and the principles of kingdom economics.

The transitional splits must be seen by kingdom leaders as economic waves of growth for God's holy time cycles. This window of accessibility will be a time of unprecedented opportunity to close the prosperity gap by the usability of kingdom economics and the desire to attain wealth now; but more importantly, for the distribution of wealth for those that might become collateral damage as a result of the unrecognized disconnect of the transitions.

The traditional church of society today has realized the need for an paradigm shift outside of the box of religion, but has been powerless to do anything about changing their plight. Here in *figure 5* we see that both the levitical priesthood and the king's office are not one and can't be. The decree is that Levi and Simon

46

be scattered and divided among there 12 brothers. The graph of *figure 5* shows the church inside the box.

In *figure 7* the graph show the paradigm shift from the human priesthood as the church (The box) to the spiritual priesthood and kingship of Melchizedek which Christ lineage as king and priest comes from; therefore the true heirs as kings is aligned with the more realistic sense and larger aspects of the ecclesia. As a matter of fact, a shift into our kingship really isn't required except to know that through Christ Jesus we were already brought forth as kings and priests as one to his God our Father. All we need to do is claim our heritage and exercise our authority right now.

Progressive Transition of the KOTP:
The 3 Levels of Priestly Transitions
1st Level: Preparation for the Holy Time Cycles

Zech. 12:7, 8; 7) ***And the Lord shall save and give the victory to the tents of Judah first, that the glory of the house of David and the glory of the inhabitants of Jerusalem may not be magnified and exalted above Judah.*** 8) <u>***In that day will the Lord guard and defend the inhabitants of Jerusalem, and he who is (spiritually) feeble and stumbles among them in that day [of persecution] shall become [strong and noble] like David; and the house of David [shall maintain its supremacy] like God, like the Angle of the Lord Who is before them It is like the dew that comes on the hills of Zion; for there the Lord has commanded the blessing, even life forevermore [upon the high and the lowly]***</u>.

2 Chron. 29:35 and also the burnt offerings were in abundance, with the fat of the peace offerings and the drink offerings for every burnt offering. So the service of the house of the Lord was set. *2 Chron. 29:34 but the priests were too few, so that they could not fray all the burnt offerings. Wherefore their brethren the Levites did help them, till the work was ended, and until the other priests had sanctified themselves: for the Levites were more upright in heart to sanctify themselves than the priests.* Josh 7:14 *Therefore you shall be brought according to your tribes. And it shall be that the tribe which the Lord takes shall <u>come according to families</u> and the family which the Lord takes <u>shall come by households</u>; and the households which the Lord takes <u>shall</u> <u>come man by man</u>.*

2nd Level: John the Baptist the Bride

Mk 1:3, 4; The voice of one crying in the wilderness prepare the way of the Lord, make his beaten path straight (level and passable). *4)* John the Baptist appeared in the wilderness (desert), preaching baptism [obligating] repentance (a change of one's mind for the better, heartily amending one's ways, with abhorrence of his past sins) in order to obtain forgiveness of and release from sins. Jn 3:29, 30; 29) He who has the bride is the bridegroom; but the groomsman who stands by and listens to him rejoices greatly and heartily on account of the bridegroom's voice. This then is my pleasure and joy, and it is now complete. *30)* He must increase, but I must decrease.

Jn 16:32 *Behold, the hour cometh, yea, is now here, that ye shall be scattered. Every man to his own home, and shall leave me alone: and yet I am not alone, because the Father is with me.*

Is 53:10-12 **yet it pleased the Lord to bruise Him**; He hath put Him to grief when thou shall make His soul an offering for sin, **He shall see His seed,** He shall prolong His days, and the pleasure of the Lord shall prosper in His hand. *11) He shall see of the travail of His soul, and shall be satisfied: by His knowledge shall My **righteous servant justify many;** for he shall bear their iniquities. 12) Therefore will I divide Him a portion with the great [kings and rulers], and **He shall divide the spoil with the strong**, because He poured out His life unto death, and was numbered with the transgressors and He bore the sin of many, and made intercession for the transgressors.*

3rd Level: The Preeminence of Melchizedek's Priesthood

*Ps 35:27 **Let them shout for joy, and be glad, that favor my righteous cause: Yea, let them say continually, "Let the Lord be magnified, which hath pleasure in the prosperity of His servant".** Zech 12:7 <u>**And the Lord shall save and give victory to the tents of Judah first, that the glory of the house of David and the glory of the inhabitants of Jerusalem may not be magnified and exalted above Judah**</u>. Jn 12:24 I assure you, most solemnly I tell you, unless a grain of wheat falls into the earth and dies, it remains [just one grain; it never becomes more but lives] by itself alone. But if it dies it produces many others and yields its rich harvest.* Heb 7:13, 14; *13)* For the one of whom these things are said belonged [not to the priestly line but] to another tribe, no member of which has officiated at the altar. *14)* For it is obvious that our Lord sprang from the tribe of Judah, and **Moses** mentioned nothing about **priest** in connection with that tribe.

48

Jn 15:2 Every branch in **Me** that have no fruit [that stops bearing] He cuts away; and He cleanses and repeatedly prunes every branch that continues to bear fruit, to make it bear more and richer and more excellent fruit. Heb 11:39, 40 And all these having obtained a good testimony through faith did not receive the promise, God having provided something better for **us**, that **they** should not be made perfect apart from **us**. Mal 3:4 **Then** the offering of Judah and Jerusalem will be pleasant to the Lord, **as in days of old, as in the former years**. Is 65:8, 9; *8)Thus said the Lord, "A new wine is found in the cluster, and one said, destroy it not for a blessing is in it: so will I do for sake of My servant, that I may not destroy them all. 9) I will bring forth a seed out of Jacob, and out of Judah an inheritor of My **mountains**: and Mine elect shall inherit it, and My **servants** shall dwell there.*

Ps 22:30, 31; *A seed or posterity of Christ shall serve Him. It shall be accounted to the Lord for a generation. 31)* They shall come and shall **declare** His righteousness unto a people yet to be born - that He has done it [that it is finished]! [Ref. Rev 1:8] Ps 24:6 This is **Jacob, the generation** of those who **seek** Him. Rev 1:6 And has made **us kings and priests** to His God and Father, to Him be glory and dominion forever and ever. Amen. Lk 22:29 And I bestow upon you a kingdom, just as My Father bestowed **one** upon Me. Rom 8:16-18 The Spirit Himself bears witness with our spirit that we are children of God and if children, then **heirs of God and joint heirs with Christ;** if indeed we suffer with Christ, that we may also be glorified together.

PROMISE PHASE 2: WORKS

Filling the Kings' Treasuries

Recognizing the city of God is like having a spiritual love affair with the word of God. The spiritual affair will help one to (meditate) or think about the word constantly as you normally would with someone you are very much in love with. The spiritual state of one's consciousness that have been enlightened will recognize the three (3) dimensional rules and its many facets of interpretations and infinite meanings. This is the climactic and the major theme behind the apocalypse and the most important in recognizing beforehand not just the perfect man within you but the works of the spirit operating through him. This is the modus operandi or operation of the spirit performing the works associated within the kingdom or the city of God proclaimed to be at hand and within us now!

Proverb 25: 1 – <u>The glory of God is to conceal a thing, but the honor of kings is to search out a matter</u>. It is by faith and not reason that one comes into this Truth. Those who find and eventually possess the **jewels** (stones) from Christ crown shall become a pillar in the foundation made in heaven; but manifested on earth. One of the reasons for possessing these precious and priceless jewels is for their spiritual attributes. <u>To spiritually display the efficacious work of unifying the multitudes of God's people as one perfect and new man.</u> The twelve (12) gates allow admission to the kingdom of God that is within you. The twelve (12) gates each one a jewel or pearl denotes "wise sayings". These jewels symbolize the priceless quality of the twelve apostles' teachings. The premise of perfection for kingdom leaders is to be humans being not humans becoming perfect. This mentality is what glorifies the perfected. All of this, the holy city and its spiritual treasuries are embodied within the incorruptible seed that we have been spiritually impregnated with.

The holy city is full of the glory of God; and wisdom has brought it forth to illuminate the spiritual consciousness of kingdom leaders with the revelation of Christ and His kingdom. Through the **vertical window** of heaven, wisdom presents the **white fields** as the divine will, thoughts, plans and promises of Christ to the minds, hearts and souls of the kingdom leaders. Possessing the infinite white fields is the key that connects the mind (which is the organ of the spirit) to the Mind of Christ and His heritage, this is the royal heritage that has been passed on though the ages. ***Allowing true kingdom leaders access to the*** *vertical window of the spirit, whosoever gather first though the spiritual and mental, not material processes shall gather fields already white for harvest. This is the wisdom of heaven, the hidden treasures of unseen dimensions of wealth that are laid up for kings to possess.*

Inevitably, an integration process of engagement must occur between the mind, heart and soul of man to the divine will, thoughts, plans and purposes of God from the spiritual gate or vertical dimension of the cube that great city of God mentioned in Rev 21:15, 16. This is the true essence of **kingdom listening** and **kingdom thinking**. When the mind, heart and soul is quickened by the spirit; as a result, the mental faculties of the man and the passions of his heart becomes qualitatively renewed, creating an inward awareness and eternal relationships with the New Jerusalem that's free from boundaries and is economically transforming! This is the integrative process that magnifies our intellectual activity, so that our three dimensional landscape can support in part, if not the full revelation of Christ bought forth by the "mother" of us all, the New Jerusalem. However, the process towards the present now is predicated on our receptivity of the spirit of truth coming to our souls though the horizontal gate.

The double edge sword which denotes the spirit of truth is crucial in expanding our mental capacity as kingdom leaders to see the fullness of Christ. The infinite workings of the double edge sword cuts and lay open the soul to the spirit. Cutting deep to convert and reconfigure our thinking by dividing in pieces what is of the flesh and what is of the spirit, with the spirit being the discerner of both the thoughts and intentions of the hearts. This is rightly dividing the word of truth between the natural man (the king) and the spiritual man (the priest).

Those whose senses and mental faculties have been trained and instructed according to the counsel of the kingdom(wisdom) will have the intellectual apprehension, with penetrating insight, to understand how to rule and demonstrate kingdom economics; yes, the physical representation of hidden riches laid up in the secret dark places. "Be ye holy" is the hallmark and epitome of working out one's salvation (claiming God's inheritance as heirs) for true kingdom leaders. The separating force of the word of truth sanctifies; while at the same time making whole though suffering, one becomes victorious by laying bear the heart and allowing the sword of Truth to remove whatever ill feelings that may have hardened the heart, mind and soul; further still, even, the dogma, traditions, layers of theological doctrine, willing ignorance, stupid foolishness and preoccupation that doesn't profit you or anyone else nothing but vain folly. It is the kingdom leader who truly lay all at the altar of truth that purifies their heart. This process seals the heart from the soil and stains of the worlds' monetary system. Love covers a multitude of sin so that the friction of world events does not grind down our affections and sensibilities toward the operations of the spirit. Love is self sacrificing; it alone bears all burdens, and suffers all trails and inflictions for God's people and for the kingdom.

In order to extract the beautiful meaning of the apocalyptic symbolism; we as kingdom leaders must first recognize that the kingdom of heaven is at hand and that it is within each and every one of God's children. Obviously, as you probably already know, faith is not based on what we see; but on what you don't see. That's why it's important to see the innermost; spiritual realities more than the visible outward evidence of symbolism.

In Rev. 21: 16 & 17: there is a beauty of perfection and completeness founded in the symbolism of the New Jerusalem. (Four means perfection in Greek and completeness in Hebrew). This shows that God's presence has always been present in Jerusalem (topographically) and that the New Jerusalem being from heaven above is free and its foundations are laid up in the counsels of eternity. Remember! Simplicity is the key; and indeed if New Jerusalem is free, one must go within thee. For, truly, the kingdom too; is inside you. When associated with the heavenly kingdom (the Cube) the apocalyptic symbolism carries enormous implications when understood three dimensionally. If kingdom leadership were to express the unseen wealth of the kingdom, then the meaning of the kingdom will have larger expressions of authority and power in our lives. If and when kingdom leaders establish **three dimensional thinking** then greater manifestations of better promises will be accelerated in our lives. If kingdom leadership were to experience the unseen wealth of the kingdom, then the meaning of the kingdom will have greater influence of authority and power in other leader's lives. This would represent the bride adorned with her jewels, which is indicative of the foundations of the holy city.

In Luke 1:41 – here is a beautiful example of the reverence for the coming of the Revelation of Christ. Elizabeth upon hearing the welcome embrace of Mary's Immaculate Conception, Elizabeth's son John leaped in her womb. This bares testimony to the illustrious light of the unveiling or Revelation of Christ appearing. Meantime, the appearing which are contained in the Revelation continues to bare witness of itself.

Now, the time after their birth, John again bears witness to the fullness of the Revelations. This shows that the illumination of the appearing continued shining forth the divine decree; hence revealing that the result of the decree is perpetual and completely still. The irony of John declaration in John 1:15 shows that the now dimensions is omnipresent and encompassing. John recognized that although Jesus was born after him, Christ preexisted before him. It's imperative that true kingdom leaders bare witness to the phenomenon of the Oneness with Christ and the fullness of His revelation. Remember "the possessor is greater that the professor". Christ understood that there wasn't any greater than John; but at the same time, John understood that he had to decrease. That is why Christ admonishes that to be greater in the kingdom of heaven you had to decrease and be the least! Decreasing to the size of a mustard seed and being less than the least literally mean dying daily to the full revelation of Christ.

Now, at this present time, as then, is the beginning of the end but not the last. This is the phenomenon that's hidden and contained in the revelation of Christ. John the Baptist being the forerunner of Jesus Christ the humbled; couldn't be forerunner for Christ Jesus the now exalted One who is to be gloried. In short, the two offices of **the king and priest** <u>**must become as one in Jesus and became 12 through his disciples which was and still is the divine government on earth**</u>;

Note! From the written law of Moses, to the prophets of the old testament who died in faith without seeing the promise; to John the Baptist of the new testament who died in Christ didn't see the kingdom; from the generation of the beginning to Abraham though the house of Jacob. This is the prophetic decreed that the royal heritage and all of its inheritance be unto Christ the King; from Christ and to Christ and through Christ shall His royal seed be manifested throughout all His seeds. He is the embodiment of the heritage of Jacob. Christ is the Branch that is imparted as the remnant seed of Jacob procreated throughout the 42nd generation to raise the foundations of many generations of kingdom leaders.

Propagating and proclaiming the prophetic decree of "**the word of God**" and "What thus said the Lord" and "He sent His word" and "the word of God came" are to impart wisdom; namely, the divine counselor to kingdom leaders heavenly calling. So all this, the perfecting of kings (kingdom leaders) is the crown jewels from Christ's crown. Indeed, this work of perfecting the kings for the kingdom bare witness that eternity truly has been placed in the divine sphere of our conscious minds. This is the place where the divine landscape of eternity, the New Jerusalem becomes the focal point in the mind, heart and soul of kingdom leaders revealing the quintessential light of truth. This is the climax of realizing and living our divine nature because what lies at that focal point is a glimpse of the divine manifold visions proceeding from God's plan of unifying his people and blessing us with the promises of our accelerated inheritance his holy time cycles. For kingdom leaders, the proleptic blueprint is the **divine power** needed to execute the glorious instructions for future promises to be manifested now, through those kingdom leaders who have and those that will overcome. This is the work that glorifies Christ Jesus and gives honor to both the Kings of Kings and his kingdom leaders!

Black Disparity and Democratic Divide

The disparities unfortunately is increasingly widening between the two extreme dissimilarities, the inherent characteristic of Satan's dichotomy. A balancing act that will not be balanced, even if a few blacks are elevated individually but represent a constituent that are not elevated both will fail and the disparity increases. Although the financial gap may seem to close for a select few individually; unfortunately, the debt system does not collectively support those that do not enter; further widening the gap which is indicative of a capitalistic system that doesn't support political or economic unity among the masses. In retrospect, this was considered a novelty as early as the 16th century. This is nothing new because when usury was introduced the concept of long-term loan soon ensued as it slowly caught on and the rulers then gradually realized that there was a market for this phenomenon.

This condition is prevalent specifically in the black community which is widening the disparity in the areas of wealth creation, economic development and social advancement for the masses within the debt system. As a result, this type of scrupulous conformity hinders the efficaciousness of leader development let along true kingdom leaders. In the work of Robert William Fogel and Eugene D. Genovese "Time on the Cross: The Economics of American Slavery" and "The Political Economy of Slavery" reveals within the world debt system how slavery and commercial agriculture was discriminately associated with the same widening disparities then, that society and capitalism are experiencing today.

Within the democratic leadership of today, blacks and their leadership are still enslaved to each other, by no fault of their own because they lack the prudence in utilizing either the principles of kingdom economics or the theories of the debt system. Society is the last to be pulled in the vortex of the debt system; and therefore will always lag behind business which will always follow capitalism which must follow the turbulent waves of the debt system. Consequently; because of this lack when you don't know what you don't know you can only perpetuate a broke mentality predicated on economic shifts that have already occurred; while trying to communicate the results of the shifts to sectors of society dependent on that leadership.

This type of mind set produce weak political leadership incapable of grappling with the overwhelming responsibility of false wealth creation in order to generate capital to deal with the inherent after affects and condition of the debt system.

Consequently, falling into a maintenance mode of fixing non-productive projects that's commonly associated with federal funded programs, not-for-profit businesses, immoral issues of sex, crime, and drug abuse resulting in pornography, same sex and alternative lifestyle issues, (STD/HIV-AIDS) disease prevention, increase of unemployment and outsourcing of jobs health issues of health care industry, Immigration issues, which is a handicap to social development and economic development. Simply put, all these programs and more are liabilities and a serious drain on capital resources that is already scarce because of the lack of government fiduciary and financial responsibilities.

So, it should be extremely clear, because the intangible aspects of the debt system it is irrespective of your status, color, creed, or religion. Rather you're a conservative or liberal, Democrat or Republican, politician, lawmaker or businessman the debt system must be fed. In other words the government must be forced to produce money but since it doesn't have any it must rely on debt capital. Simply put, if the government does not produce money it must continual to raise taxes or cut these federally funded programs when federal spending stops or use capital reserves such as our entitlement if the need arises and it will! So here again lies the central activity of the diabolical dichotomy, where two opposing interest clings tenaciously to one another or some other schism.

Weak political leadership is hampered also by a people that have developed a welfare-dependent mindset and overindulgence in non-productive activity that doesn't produce economic, political or social advancements but instead is mentally lackadaisical toward any attempt of personal improvement; while reflecting hostility and contempt toward the handicapped leadership for seemingly not addressing insurmountable issues that threaten their freedom from dependency. This fact illustrates the importance of economic independence for African Americans and society as a whole. This would be the challenge for the new breed of wealthy blacks who have collectively developed the financial astuteness and political savvy in their elevation into the class of wealth creation for the masses.

Super Symbolic Immaterial Dimension

This unprincipled condition of this divide played out over a long period since Satan slammed into the earth, his debt system have imperceptibly evolved under the inattentive eye of society; while the economic elements are becoming super symbolic it is also transposing itself within the immaterial dimensions of technology. Technology is accelerating the secular culture transition into the debt system; but on the other hand, it is impeding the religious aspects of the church in its spiritual transformation toward kingdom economics and is descending more towards the dependency of the debt system. Consequently, the economics intrusion of this partnership became demanding and pressing creating a separation; which in turn corresponded to deep crises of mental repression. Reducing the church to a position of subjection to the government; eventually harboring acquiescence hostility of unfulfilled promises.

Unfortunately, this explains the church reluctant conformity to transition from the mind set of the world for tangible possession to a kingdom mind set of intangible blessings, which entails having spiritual authority over God's holy time cycle and than having its promises manifested against the world debt system.

Capitalism-Black Advancement

Blacks who are already financially and socially advanced will eventually be forced to participate at higher levels of the world economy because massive amounts of accumulated capital (entitlements) must eventually be pushed into circulation for huge profits creation throughout society. Capitalism will move into those sections of black communities where leadership, economic and political development are matured. Those astute blacks who established a socio-economic leadership base and the next generation of black leaders should be especially active in successive leadership development; providing the financial support systems that is attached to the capital structure of kingdom economics will reap increased economic and personal freedom. The social aspect of life is drastically improved only when implementation of any leadership development program is integrated into the principles of kingdom leadership according to biblical standards; which extend way beyond any secular leadership base and eventually stagnates over time within the debt system.

The greatest challenge now for the emerging black leadership is to position the next generations of kingdom leaders for the financial shifts that is occurring.

Kingdom leadership that have shifted their paradigm accordingly from the world economic system to the kingdom economic system will be positioned properly to build upon the foundation of God's kingdom and utilize the principles of kingdom economics which; will be the financial support and hedge of protection for when the market shift to the personal accounts as the ownership society; while at the same time, generating the economic cycles that will raise the socio-economic standard of the masses who choices to participates. How does one then visualize the higher dimensions of the unknown beyond what they are comfortable with, if all they know is what they know? In other words, do you know more than what you don't know? From an economical standpoint, Satan's world debt system has embedded itself in the minds of society today, it is the only system we've become accustom to and know.

Society and particularly the church are lacking a radically new physical picture of kingdom economics; mainly because it exceeds the capabilities of the human mind to grasp the powerful economic phenomenon of exponential unification. The unseen dimensions of wealth are not associated with the out of reach future as is commonly lived, but the now, which is a higher dimension of simplicity is attainable by integrating the past and future into a coherent single picture of timeless existence through God's holy time cycles. This type of vision could only become practically established according to kingdom economics. We must make the mental shift to the now since all we have is just now. The present moment that is outside of our limited preoccupation with the past and the ardent desire of a future heaven. This mental shift basically frees the mind of the restraints of one dimension thinking that is normally associated with the material realm of earth time and everything and their affects that's attached to it (community, investing, property, financing, jobs, credit, debt, interest etc.). Still the essential factor that remains is the great anticipation, expectation and awareness of true wealth creation that comes when we visualize the unifying cycles of God's unseen wealth is what makes the power of kingdom economics so awesome; because at the higher levels, time and space are turned into each other creating timelessness for us.

However, the rules of kingdom economics seem antiquated next to the existing monetary system of today and its overwhelming influence over the world. Regardless of how powerful the debt system may seem to be, kingdom leaders must never forget that the regressive characteristic of the world financial system is to implode and explode. The activity of Satan's debt cycles is always operating on the periphery of the eternal economy of grace and is encompassed within a secondary cycle outside of God's holy time cycles as either epicycloids or hypocycloids. Ironically, those within societies who seem to be advancing financially through the world system are actually operating outside of kingdom economics this includes the church too. The powerful and unifying forces of God's economy of grace only becomes visible as the operations of the blessings though our promises are matured in us as a witness of evidence for Christ in the world.

The time will come when kingdom leaders should redeem their holy times cycles and rupture from the past beyond the debt system into the higher dimensions where the storehouse of God's holy time cycles are locked up in the kingdom of heaven. Once kingdom leadership are mentally enlightened to a realistic picture of true freedom and wealth creation and what its promises look like; then the liberating operation of the kingdom will work through them to become an practical model for an exodus freeing generations from the confinements of the debt system.

Foreigner Advancement

Unlike many other foreigners who was once outcast have accessed and is utilizing the debt system; blacks have continually been denied access and control of the same debt system by those who was once outcast. African Americans are looking to enter also knocking at the doors of the federal government just as they did in 1865 and 1866. This is the same system before America was discovered that was eventually inherited by foreigners in Europe. Blacks, like any other Christian consider themselves chosen of God and find themselves in the same scenario just as the Jews-the chosen of God, with the only difference being they knew about the prohibition of usury but used the illegitimate system anyway. But when you have been labeled an outcast and accustom to hardship and hostility including murders and the annihilation of millions, any opportunity to advance financially seems like a blessing even if it is destructive to society.

Eventually, the Jews developed and controlled the financial institution of money-lending once they had moved into the upper ranks of the political and capitalistic elite. Unfortunately blacks, like the other foreigners, without any alternative will be forced to participate politically within the debt system; especially during the massive intrusion of illegal immigrants to participate in the capitalistic debt system of America. By becoming an American citizen immigrants want the opportunities that this country has always offered to outsiders including free education, job opportunities, paying taxes, free health

58

care, have all been unresolved issues of immigration reform have laid dormant for decades erupted on May 1, 2006 as the Day of the Immigrant.

We are starting to see the progressive aspects of unresolved issues and their affect upon other unresolved issues associated with it such as entitlements. Entitlements are a transposition of slavery as a continuous psychological form of dependency. Slavery today has become an immaterial property of attachment; because of its attachment to the intangible medium of exchange though the symbolic debt system. In other words, jobs financially support the entitlement, retirement and social security programs and immigration reform and the immigrants will play a major role and have huge political and economic implications in the near future for the democratic party.

PROMISE PHASE 2: WORKS
Power of Submission: Die in Christ

Jn 6:28, 29 <u>They then said, What are we to **do**, that we may [**habitually**] be working **the works** of God?</u> [<u>What are we to do to carry out what God requires?</u>] *29)* Jesus replied, This is the **work** (service) that God asks of you: <u>that you **believe** in the One</u> Whom He has sent [that you cleave to, trust, rely on, and have **faith** in His Messenger]. Jn 9:4 **We must work the works** of Him who sent Me and **be busy with His business** while it is daylight; **night is coming on, when no man can work**. 1 Cor 15:27, 28 For He hath put **all** things **under His feet**. But when he said **all** things are put in **subjection** [under Him], it is evident that he [Himself] is excepted who does the **subjecting** of **all** things to him. *28)* However, when everything is **subjected** to him, then the Son himself will also **subject** himself to [the Father] who put **all** things under him, so that God **may be all in all** [be everything to everyone, supreme, the <u>indwelling and controlling factor of life</u>]. [Ref. Jn 17:13]; Eph 4:1, 3-6 *1)* I therefore, a prisoner of the Lord, beseech you that ye walk worthy of the vocation wherewith ye are called. *3)* <u>Be eager and strive earnestly to guard and keep the harmony and **oneness** of [**and produced by**] the Spirit in the binding power of peace</u>. *4)* There is **one** body, and **one** spirit, even as ye are called in **one** hope of your calling. *5)* **One** Lord, **one** faith, **one** baptism. *6)* **One** God and Father of us **all**, Who is above **all** [Sovereign over **all**], pervading **all** and [living] in [us] **all**. Eph 4:23, 24; *23)* **And be constantly renewed in the spirit of your mind** [having a fresh mental and spiritual attitude]. *24)* and that ye put on the **new man**, which after God is created in righteousness and true holiness. Heb 6:1 <u>Therefore let us go on and get past the elementary stage in the</u>

teachings and doctrine of Christ (the Messiah), advancing steadily toward the completeness and perfection that belong to spiritual maturity. Let us not again be laying foundation of **repentance and abandonment of dead works** and of **faith** toward God.

Divine Measurement of Accelerated Works
Times of Refreshing

Rev 1:8 I am the Alpha and the Omega, the Beginning and the End, says the Lord God, He who is and Who was and Who is to come, the Almighty (the ruler of all) [Ref. Is 9:6]; Mt 9:37, 38; 37) Then said he unto the disciples, The harvest truly is plentiful, **but the laborers are few**.

Jn 4:32 But He said unto them, I have meat or food [nourishment] to eat of which you know nothing and have no idea of: As the Samaritan woman didn't understand the **switch** from physical water to **spiritual eternal life** (4:15), neither did the disciples understand the **switch** from physical food to **spiritual food**. These are instances of spiritual dullness. In 2:20 it was the Jews. In 3:4 it was Nicodemus; in 4:11 the Samaritan woman and now the disciples (11:12, 14:5)

Jn 4:34 Jesus said to them, My food [nourishment] is to do the will & pleasure of God **Who** sent **Me** and to accomplish and completely finish **His** work: This food is not simply knowing the will of God, **but doing it**. It is **practice or output** (1 Cor 3:1-3); (Heb 5:12-14). In v. 32 Jesus referred to the food He had and in this verse He tells what it is, namely, **doing the will of His Father**. Notice the difference between **milk** and **solid food**. Heb5:12 For even though by this time you ought to be teaching others, **you actually need someone to teach you over again the very first principles of God's Word. You have come to need mild not solid food**:

This verse suggests all believers ought to be teachers not in the formal sense, but in the sense that those who have been taught ought to **impart** to others what they have learned through the experience and practice of bearing good fruit that God has given them. **The first principles** are the elements out of which everything else is built on. Have come to need: they have regressed because of disuse. If you don't practice what you see or hear, you lose it and have to be told it again and again. To not use it is to lose it. [milk …solid food]: The author illustrates the ingredients of growth. **Milk equals input**. **Solid food equals output**. We start with the input of truth (1 Pe 2:2), exercising the readiness of learning. We gradually implement the **principle of practice** for retention of truth. <u>Consistent and persistent **practice of truth** results in growth to maturity.</u> **Milk is information or input but food is practice or output.** Too often we stop with input rather that going on to output or productivity.

Jn 4:35 Do you not say, It is still four months until harvest time comes? **Look! I tell you, raise your eyes and observe** [discern] the fields and see how they already white for harvest. **Jn 4:35, 38;** *35)* Do you say, It is still four months until harvest time comes? Look! **I tell you, raise your eyes and observe (think) the fields and see how they are already white for harvesting.** *38)* I sent you [all] to reap a crop for which you have not **toiled**. Other men have **labored** and you have stepped in to reap the results of their **works**.

Note! **Jn 4:35** In v. 35-38 Jesus puts before his disciples an opportunity not only to teach a fundamental kingdom principle of "**doing**" but create an anticipation that he has already produced for them that they weren't even aware of. This would become "**food**" for them if they take advantage of it. The 1st part of v. 35 has been taken as an actual fact of the traditional 4 month Passover harvest. If this is factual, then this conversation took place in December/January because the harvest began in the middle of April. Actually, Christ is speaking about the approaching Samaritans. In them He sees a spiritual harvest opportunity for which his disciples will not have to wait long. The 12 disciples represent Christ kingdom structure on earth; therefore, the spiritual principles are already exceedingly and abundantly working within his structure. So the 2nd halve of verse 35 show how the **rhema** word of Jesus when spoken redirected our traditional thinking away from the accustom facts to renewed practical experiences faith. The fields wave its white harvest, look for the spiritually mature laborers that are strong, the rich fruits are ripe and the storehouses are ready: pray you therefore the **Lord of the harvest** to send forth the **remnant seeds of Christ**-the laborers of a perfected sort, and gather the fruit for the world. This reaping of the harvest is by mental not material processes. The laborers are certainly few in the vineyard of Mind-sowing and reaping.

Jn 4:36 The Reaper of a spiritual harvest receives wages – that is, fruit which brings joy. In this case, **Jesus sowed by giving the <u>message</u> to the woman. He was about to reap because He would see the whole city saved.** <u>Also</u> the disciples were going to reap the harvest that Christ has sown. Note the "**hundred**" wages Jesus promises in Mt. 19:27-29 (1 Cor 3:6-8; 2 Cor 5:10). Jn 4:37 One sows…another reaps: a vital lesson in establishing **kingdom economics** for his still spiritually immature disciples. There are various tasks and laborers in the work of the Lord, but all receive honor alike

Jon 1:17 Now the Lord had prepared and appointed a great fish to swallow up Jonah. And Jonah was in the belly of the fish three days and three nights. [Ref. Mt. 12:40] Jon 2:6 I went down to the bottoms of the mountains that rise from off the ocean floor. I was locked out of life and imprisoned in the land of death. Here is two examples how God shortens the future to your present state of consciousness or lengthens your present state of consciousness to the future.

Note: **Eccl 3:11 states that God put eternity in our hearts and mind meaning we can decree and determine through our eternal view of the now and control the points of times to our present state of being. Literally God eternal promises or His seasonal cycles brought forth to fruition now!**

Ps 90:4 For a thousand years in Your sight are but as yesterday when it is past, or as a watch in the night. 2 Pe 3:9 The Lord is not slack - does not delay and is not tardy or slow about what He promises, ..., but that all should turn to repentance.

Definition: Let's take a look at this word "white" *3022 Leukos*-lyoo-kos (*"light"*); **white**. 216 *illumination* OWR, ORE; from 215-**"to be"** (make) *"luminous"* (in every sense including: day, sun, daylight, daybreak, life, salvation, prosperity, wisdom and justice, light, brightness, sunlight, enlightening, happiness, cheerfulness. Ore is closely related to life and happiness, not walking in the shadow of the valley of death. Light is symbolic of prosperity. And often used as an indicator of time. Then their "stars of light" (Ps 148:3). Like a clock they regulate the seasons. Metaphorically or literally God is closely associated with light and prominent metaphoric meaning is **"instruction"** (Prov 6:23). *2312 Theodidaktos* Theh-od-d-ak-tos *divinely instructed:* taught of God *3129 Manthano* to learn from, to endeavor, to desire, to seek, to learn, experience, bring into experience, to have learned and to teach instruction concerning the facts and plan of salvation. To cause oneself to know more fully with a moral bearing and responsibility (Jn 6:45); the capacity of knowing *3854 lahag*, lah-hag *to be eager;* intense mental application of study. *1922 epiginosko*, ep-ig-in-oce-ko; recognize, **to become fully acquainted with**, to acknowledge with meaning of clear and exact knowledge. (Epignosis) expresses a more thorough participation in the object of knowledge or part of the subject, and always refers to knowledge which has very powerful influences on the form of the spiritual and religious life, a knowledge laying claim to personal sensitivity and exerting an influence upon the person. It proves the relation of the person's knowing of the object of his knowledge base. [Ref. Col 3:10]. It means the discernment in connection with the knowledge of possession of salvation which determines the moral conduct and enables one to avoid errors. *4908 Sunetos* soon-et-os; insight, the critical faculty of how to evaluate people, things and circumstances [Ref. Eph

3:4]. penetrating acute mental discernment, practical sense of things. ***Definition: 4920 Suniemi***, soon-ee-ay-mee to *comprehend* to bring together. When the word is confined to the sphere of mental perception, it means to hear, notice, perceive, recognize, understand, put something together and make sense out of it. It's like **collecting together the individual features of an object into a whole. Suniemi involves the activity of knowing**.

Eph 1:18 By having the **eyes of your heart flooded with light**, so that you can know and understand the hope to which He has called you, and how rich is His glorious inheritance in the saints. **His set apart ones.**

1 Cor 2:7 But what we are setting forth is a wisdom of God once **hidden [from the human understanding] and now revealed to us by God - [that wisdom] which God devised and decreed before the ages for our glorification [to lift us into the glory of His presence]**.

Rom 8:17, 18; 17) And if children, then heirs; heirs of God, and joint-heirs with Christ; if so be that we suffer with Him, **that we may be also glorified together**. 18) For I consider that the suffering of this present time are not worth being compared with the **glory that is about to be revealed to us and in us and for us and conferred on us**.

Ps 8:3, 6; 3)When I view and consider Your heavens, **the works of Your fingers,** the moon and the stars which You have ordained and established. 6) You made him to have dominion over the **works of Your hands**; You have put all things under his feet:

Jn 5:20 The Father clearly loves the Son and discloses to (shows) Him everything that He Himself does. And He will disclose to Him (let Him see) greater things yet than these, so that you may marvel and be full of wonder and astonishment.

Jn 14:12 Verily, verily I say to you, He that **believeth** on Me, the **works that I do shall he do also and greater works than these shall he do**; because I go unto My Father. **Dut 8:18 But thou shalt remember the Lord thy God: for it is he that giveth thee power to get wealth, that He may establish His covenant which he swore unto your fathers, as it is this day.**

1 Cor 10:24 Let no man seek his own, but every man another's wealth.

Gal 5:13 For you brethen, were [indeed] called to freedom; only [do not let your] freedom be an incentive to your flesh and an opportunity or excuse [for selfishness], **but through love you should serve one another**.

Rom 3:26 **It was to demonstrate and prove at the present time** (in the now season) that He justifies and accepts as righteous him who has [true] faith in Jesus. Ps 105: 43, 44; And He brought forth His people with joy, and His chosen ones with gladness and singing. *44)* And gave them the lands of the nations [of Canaan], **and reaped the fruits of those peoples' labors.**

Rom 11:2-5 No, God has not rejected and discounted His people [whose destiny] He had marked out and appointed and foreknew from the beginning. Do you know what the scriptures says of Elijah, how he pleads with God against Israel? 3) Lord, they have killed Your prophets; they have demolished Your altars. And I alone am left, and they seek my life. 4) But what is God's reply to him? **I have kept for Myself seven thousand (7,000) men who have not bowed the knee to Baal! 5) Even so then at this present time there are remnant seeds** (a small believing minority), selected (chosen) by grace (by God's unmerited favor and graciousness). Is 60:22 A little one shall become a thousand and a small one a strong nation. I the Lord will hasten it in its time.

Rom 15:16 In making me a minister of Christ Jesus to the Gentiles. I act in the priestly service of the Gospel (the good news) of God, in order that the **sacrificial offering of the Gentiles** may be acceptable [to God], consecrated and made holy by the Holy Spirit.

Jn 4:35 Look! I tell you, raise your eyes and observe (comprehend) the fields and see how they are already white for harvesting.

Rom 8:28, 29; We are assured and know that [**God being a partner in their labor beforehand**], all things **work together** [and are fitted into a plan] **for good to and for those who love God and are called according to His design and purpose.** *29)* For those whom He foreknew [of whom He was aware and loved beforehand], He also destined from the beginning [foreordained them] to be molded into the image of His Son [and share inwardly His likeness], that He might become the firstborn among many brethren. Rev 5:11 And I beheld, and I heard the voice of many angels round about the throne and the beasts and the elders: and the number of them was **10,000s times 10,000s, plus 1,000s of 1,000s**. [Ref. Rev 5:6].

Heb 4:3, 9; *3)* For we who have believed (adhered to and trusted in and relied on God) do enter that rest, in accordance with His declaration that those [who did not believe] should not enter when He said, as I swore in My wrath, they shall not enter My rest; **and this He said although [His] works had been completed and prepared [and waiting for all who would believe] from the foundation of the world.** *9)* So then, **there is still awaiting a full and complete Sabbath-rest reserved for the [true] people of God**; Heb 4:10, 11 10) For he who has once entered [God's] rest also has ceased from [weariness and pain] of human labors, just as God rested from those labors peculiarly His own. *11)* Let us therefore be zealous and exert ourselves and strive diligently to enter that rest [of God, to know and experience it for ourselves], that no one may fall or perish by the same kind of unbelief and disobedience [into which those in the wilderness fell].

Rom 4:5, 6; But to one who, not working (by the Law), <u>trusts (believes fully) in Him</u> Who **justifies** the ungodly, his **faith** is credited to him as righteousness (the standing <u>acceptable to God</u>). *6)* Even as David also describeth or congratulates the man and pronounces a blessing on him to whom God credits righteousness **apart from the works he does**.

Rom 11:6 But if it is by **grace** (His unmerited favor and graciousness), <u>it is no longer</u> conditioned on **works or anything men have done**. Otherwise, **grace would no longer be grace** [it would be meaningless].

Rom 3:3 What if some did not believe and were without faith? Does their lack of faith and their faithlessness nullify and make ineffective and void the faithfulness of God and His fidelity [to His Word]?

Jn 14:8-11; Philip saith unto him, Lord, show us the Father-then we will be satisfied. *9)* Jesus replied, have I been with all of you for so long of time, and do you not recognize and know me yet, Philip? <u>Anyone who has seen **Me** has seen the Father</u>. How can you say the, show us the Father? *10)* **<u>Do you not believe</u>** <u>that I am in the Father, and</u> <u>that the Father is in Me</u>? What I am telling you I do not say on My own authority and of My own accord: **but the Father Who lives continually in Me does the (His) works** (<u>His own miracles, deeds of power</u>). *11)* **Believe Me that I am in the Father and the Father in Me**; or else believe Me for the very **works** themselves. [If you cannot trust Me, at least let these **works** that I do in My Father's name convince you.]

Jn 15:7, 8; If you live in Me [**<u>abide vitally united to me</u>**] **and my words remain in you and continue to live in your hearts**, ask whatever you will, and it shall be done for you. *8)* **<u>When you bear (produce) much fruit, My Father is honored and glorified, and you show yourselves to be true followers of mine</u>**.

Rom 5:20, 21; 20) But then Law came in, [only to expand and increase the trespass making it more apparent and exciting opposition]. But where sin increased and abounded, **grace** (God's unmerited favor) **has surpassed it and increased the more and super- abounded,** 21) So that, just as sin reigned in death, [so] **grace** (His unearned and deserved favor) might reign also through righteousness (right standing with God) which issues in eternal life through Christ (the Messiah, the Anointed One Lord.

Jn 4:38 I sent you to reap a crop for which you have not **toiled**. Other men have **labored** and you have stepped in to reap the results of their **work**.

Mt 25:24-29; 24) He who had received one talent also came forward, saying, Master, I knew you to be a harsh and hard man, **reaping where you did not sow,**

and gathering where you did not winnowed or scattered [the seed]. 25) So I was afraid, and I went and hid your talent in the ground. Here you have what is your own. 27) Then you should have invested my money with the bankers, and at my coming I would have received what was my own **with interest**. 28) So take the talent away from him and give it to the one who has the ten talents. 29) For unto everyone who **has** will more be given, and he will be furnished richly so that he will have an abundance**; but from the one who does not have, even what he does have will be taken away**. Heb 5:13; For everyone who continues to feed on milk is obviously inexperienced and unskilled in the doctrine or Word of righteousness (of conformity to the divine will in purpose, thought, and action, for he is a mere infant [not able to talk yet]!

Definition: 2872 Toil kopaio, kop-ee-ah-o from 2873 to *feel fatigue, to work hard*:-(bestow) labour, be wearied. (reducing the strength) pains:-labour, trouble, weariness. 1754 energeia en-erg-i-ah efficiency ("energy"):-operation, strong, (effectual) working, to be active, efficient:-do, (be) effectual fervent, be mighty in, show forth self, work.

Col 1:29 For this I **labor** [unto weariness], striving with all the superhuman energy which He so mightily enkindles and **works** within me.

Definition: 4704 spoudazo spoo-dad-zo from *4710*; to use speed, to make effort, be prompt or earnest:-do give diligence, be diligent (forward), endeavor, labor, study, energetic, earnest:-business, carefulness, haste. *2041* work ergon, er-gon; to work, **toil**, an act, deed; The general object or result of doing and working, an object or result whose attainment or realization is not accomplished by a single act but by accumulated labor and continued work.

Heb 12:1 Therefore then, since we are surrounded by so great a cloud of witnesses [who have borne testimony to the Truth], let us strip off and throw aside every encumbrance (unnecessary weight) and that **sin** which so readily (deftly and cleverly) clings to and entangles us, and let **run** with patient endurance and steady and active persistence the appointed course of the race that is set before us. 1 Cor. 3:12, 13, 15; 12) Now if any man build upon this foundation gold, silver, precious stones, wood, hay, stubble; 13) Every man's **work** shall be made manifest: for the **day** shall declare it, because it is revealed by fire, and the fire shall try every man's work of what sort it is. 15) If any man's **work** shall be burned, he shall suffer loss: but he shall be saved; yet so as by fire. Mt 22:11-14; 11) But when the king came in to view the guests, he looked intently at a man there who had on no wedding garment. 12) And he said, friend, how did you come in here without putting on the wedding garment? And he was speechless. 13) Then the king said to the attendants, tie him hand and foot, and throw him into the darkness outside; there will be weeping and grinding of teeth. 14) For many are called (invited and summoned) but few are chosen.

Rev 3:17, 18; For you say, I am rich, I have prospered and grown wealthy, and I am in need of nothing; and you do not realize and understand that you are wretched, pitiable, poor, blind, and naked. 18) Therefore I counsel you to purchase from Me gold refined and tested by fire, that you may be [truly] wealthy, and white clothes to clothe you and to keep the shame of your nudity from being seen, and salve to put on your eyes, that you may see. Rev 14:13 Then I heard further [perceiving the distinct words of] a voice from heaven saying, Write this: Blessed are the dead from now on who die in the Lord! <u>Yes, blessed (happy, to be envied indeed), says the spirit, [in] that they may rest from their</u> **labors,** for their **works** (deeds) do follow (attend, accompany) them!

Rev 16:15 Behold, I am going to come like a thief! Blessed (happy, to be envied) is he who stays awake (alert) and who guards his clothes, so that he may not be **naked** and seen exposed!

KINGSHIP + 12 TRIBES = 60 FOLD Harvest

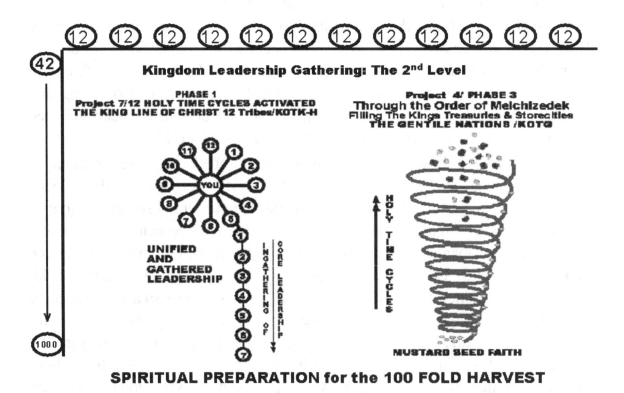

SPIRITUAL PREPARATION for the 100 FOLD HARVEST

Figure 6

FIGURE 6 GRAPH EXPLANATION

How can a nation be built from the remnant seed of Jacob in a day? You probably asking yourself, whoever heard of such a thing? You probably haven't heard, but yes; only if the spiritual blueprint of the DNA of Christ, is understood and objectified between our mental disconnects, in bringing about your heritage as it relates to both kingdom leadership and kingdom economics. Once this spiritual blueprint has become materialized and implemented in our system, it can produce an ubiquitous phenomenon, that can be manifested and fulfilled through the kings of Christ!

Are you a king? Do you know you are a king? Where are the kings? What are we heirs to? Who are these "we the people" and are they sovereign? How does royalty look today? Why must the priesthood and the kingship become one? What good will it do me to know about it? How do the kings transform today's economic landscape from a symbolic or abstract state into an actual present reality according to our kingly heritage? These propose inquiries are intuitively implicit and altogether too overwhelming to be recognized, showing that the prophetic blueprint, emblematically is seldom seen or practically understood even when it is materialized; which is kept a mystery even from His kings who are the apple of His eye and His church. When divine intensity or the fullness of the times becomes a one day blessing of grace; then, glory will be to God when the apple of His eye are magnified. Consequently, from a kingdom perspective, the economic manifestations and its implications behind how God is to be glorified today, seems problematic for the nations, because they don't see the kingdom as at hand, or it is mentally kept locked up either in the past or future, by both the church and by default, His kingdom leadership. The answers to these type of rhetorical questions are only known to kings, and are found in the quintessence of Christ ubiquitous expression of His sovereignty.

But it will become clear, when both the priesthood (the church) and the kings come to this turning point, marking a new beginning where they can start to look together as one, outside of their individual realms. There must be a major shift from a microcosmic or mustard seed perspective; to one of a macro cosmic scope. Constituting them to look from the smaller aspect of their distinct entities (phases 1 and 2) to outside of themselves into phase 3 the larger aspect within the DNA of Christ. In other words, once your mental capacity becomes focused on the present existence of Christ appearing, rather than the time Jesus appeared in time past; then the unveiling of Christ fulness is ubiquitously manifested throughout all of our kingships, which is the promises of our circles. When the sovereign power of God is used by His kings; then our authority can instantly becomes a manifestation of **divine intensity** inherent to our ubiquitous phenomenon, which is found when we introduce the DNA of Christ into the marketplace circle 42. Ref. *Figures 1, 3 & 8* but esp. *figures 6 & 8.*

When the mediation of the DNA of Christ comes between the extremes of the disconnects of the priesthood and the kingship; God will release a ubiquitous process of integration within all the mediation points, designed to galvanize horizontally multitudes of kingdom leaders into promise phase 1 kingdom structures shown in *figures 3, & 6.* This is the threshold where all three promise phase 1 of unity, promise phase 2 of work, and promise phase 3 of time are consummated at each turning point of transition. These reference points are instances of time, where Christ suddenly reestablishes the multiplicity of His spiritual kingships and the activation of His kingdom leadership. Those who were already spiritually prepared in restructuring the social fabric according to the kingdom blueprint are immediately becoming the social architects in society as the integrators or (masters of the assemblies) of today.

The divine interposition of His kings is adorned and embellished with the fullness of Christ's heritage. We have become arrayed with spiritual qualities resembling rubies, pearls, emeralds, and diamonds representing various levels of spiritual knowledge needed for seizing this kingly heritage. This priceless inheritance entails hidden dimensions of wealth, which has been transmuted into its financial equivalent and transposed into a ubiquitous platform for distribution. These modernized platforms and their channels of distribution are infused with phenomenal levels and phases of accession; which are designed to create accelerated implosions of integrated wealth, which is redistributed (the 30, 60 fold harvest that is equivalent to 1,000% to 5,000% payout) 1st to the smaller or 3rd part of the DNA of Christ, that being the remnant seeds of the king line, to be a radiant light and blessing to the much larger aspect of the kingdom the nations.

The prophetic blueprint of the DNA of Christ can only be implemented and fulfilled by the entity of the kings and their kingdom leadership. By the DNA of Christ the coronation of Christ's king seed is consecrated through the spiritual entity of the church now as one; which is now superimposed into and operating through the priesthood and kingship of Melchizedek, the power of Christ enacted through us, His kings. Like a mustard seed; the king seed of Christ blossoms into the plurality of Christ's majesty, revealing its attribute as the plurality of intensity. This attribute of divine intensity is inherent throughout the king seed line and the DNA of Christ and inevitably to the nations for their glorification. But when extended, it produces an even greater national coronation within all nations that become married to it, and fashioning anew, as one unified humanity, while releasing its glorification upon many peoples that has been integrated into the DNA of Christ. When this occur this ubiquitous blessing will produce a great influxes of wealth from the nations back into the entire structure of the DNA of Christ in circle 42.

God is eternal; and Christ inhabits eternity, and He has put eternity in our hearts; therefore, allowing us as integrators to regulate our relations with Christ and activate the courses and movements of the heavens. Also, allowing the kings to transcend the disconnects and time restraints into life of timeless reality and actuate covenant relationship that is magnified among the nations who seeks freedom. His decree stands fixed without change forever, It is Christ, who laid the foundations of the earth and filled it with incalculable wealth, because Jesus kingdom (has) come and our Father's will (has been done). But now, Christ kingdom is come it is ever present; and today both of their wills are being done on earth even as it is in heaven, through His kings for the coronation of the nations to be born in one day.

Second Level of Predestination: Sonship
Christ Glorified Through Men

Rev 1:8 I am the Alpha and Omega, the Beginning and the Ending.

Definition: Alpha (1) the first letter of the Greek alphabet so in many words beginning with this letter means Union. 260 hama-ham-ah at the "same" time, denoting close association: also, and, together, with. 746 Beginning commencement, chief, various application of order, time, place or rank: corner, at the, the first estate, magistrate, power, principality, principle, rule to be first in political power in rank and power, reign rule over; 3246 began yecud yes-ood; from 3245 a foundation, fig. beginning: x began. 3245 to set, to found intens. to found; reflex. To sit down together, settle, consult: appoint, take counsel, establish, lay the, lay for a found -ation, instruct, lay, ordain, set, sure. The infinite has no beginning which signifies the only. The truth has no beginning nor ending.

Heb 7:3 Without father without mother or ancestral line, neither with beginning of days nor ending of life, but, resembling the son of God, he continue to be a priest without interruption and without successor.

Rom 16:15 To God only wise, be glory through Jesus Christ for ever, Amen.

Definition: 5348 phthano fthan-o to be before hand, anticipate or precede; to have arrived at: (already) attained, prevent, come. 2235 Already ede-ay-day from 2228 or possibly 2229 -assuredly surely and 1211 emphasis & explicitness, now, then, also doubtless, therefore, even, already, not already, truly, verily. Already,

70

synonyms: previously, before hand, before now, yet by this time, by that time, here and now, now. 3568 Now nun, noon; particle of present time; now, present or immediate, at present: just now, this time. Before the present. 3605 all Kol, Kole Hebrew, from 3634, the whole; hence all, any, every, altogether, enough, every one, place, thing, as many as, what or whosoever, in all manner; 3634 Kalal; kaw-lal prim, root; to complete: (make) perfect.

Definition: 3956 pas, all, any every, all manner of, means always x daily, ever, every one, way + no thing - thoroughly whole. 3918 Present pareimi parimee from 3849 to be near, at hand, time being or property, be here present. At or in the vicinity of, in the proximity of. 1764 to place on hand, impend -ing, be instant: come to be at hand, present; 1722 fixed position in place, time or stare, instrumentality (medially or middle or constructively) a relation of rest, intermediate between 1510 and 1537; "in", at, rarely used with verbs of motion and then not to indicate direction. 3936 paristano, par-is-tay-mee; from 3844 to exhibit, substantiate; (instrans.), to be at hand (or ready), aid: assist, bring before, command, give presenting, prove.

Definition: Generation DHOR-1755 a root from 1752 gyrate-to move in a circle or spiral, surround or around a fixed point; a full cycle - 360 degree, a motion of time (DHOR) refers to a revolution circular motion. The period of a man's life, generation, age, race, class of men, Note: Genea contemporaries belonging to the same time existing or occurring at the same time with another or others, synchronous, co-eternal, co-instantaneous, present, age, modern. DHOR: The essence therefore is the cycle of a man's lifetime - The conception and birth of a man until the conception and birth of his offspring. Note: Mt 1:17 Christ didn't have any offspring eventually used to describe extended time periods - This demonstrates that revelation presents time as linear and measurable. For revelation is revealed to us horizontally and vertically manifested simultaneously through the true worshippers [the kings, heirs and sons].

Dut 29:29 The secret things belong unto the Lord our God, But the things which are revealed belong to us and to our children forever, that we may do all of the words of this law.

1 Cor 3:2-4; I have fed you with milk, and not with meat: for you were not yet strong enough [to be ready for it] but even yet now, you are not strong enough [to be ready for it]. 3) For you are still [unspiritual, having the nature] of the flesh. For as long as [there are] envying and jealousy and wrangling and divisions among you, are you not unspiritual and of the flesh, behaving yourselves after a human standard and like mere men? 4) For when one says, I belong to Paul, and another, I belong to Apollos, are you not proving yourselves ordinary (unchanged) men?

Acts 17:26 And He made from **one** [common origin, one source, one blood] all nations of men to settle on the face of the earth, <u>having definitely determined appointed</u> seasons [**and he has given to each the cycles it was to pass through**] and their territorial boundaries (their settlements, lands, and abodes). Ecc 3:11 He has made everything beautiful in its time. **He also has planted eternity in men's hearts and minds** [a divinely implanted sense of a purpose working through the ages which nothing under the sun but God alone can satisfy] so that no man can find out the work that God maked from the beginning to ending.

2 Peter 3:8 Nevertheless, do not let this **one** fact escape you, beloved, that with the Lord **one** (1) day. Heb 11:13 **These all died in faith not having received the promises**, <u>but having seen them afar off, and were persuaded of them</u>, and embraced them, and confessed that they were strangers and pilgrims on the earth.

Heb 11:40 Because God had **us** in mind and had something better and a greater view for us, so that they [these heroes and heroines of faith] **should not come to perfection apart from us** [before we could join them].

Heb 12:23 And to the church (assembly) of the first born who are registered [as citizens] in heaven and to the God Who is Judge of all, and to the **spirits** of the righteous (the redeemed in heaven) <u>who have been made perfect</u>.

Eph 2:14 For He is [Himself] our peace (our bond of unity and harmony), He has made us both [Jew and Gentile] **one** [body] and has broken down (destroyed, abolished) the hostile dividing wall between us.

Definition! *3423* **Heir** yaresh yaw-raysh; to *occupy* (by driving out previous tenants and possessing their place); **to** *seize*, to *rob*, to *expel*, to *impoverish*, **drive-out**, possess, seize upon take, succeed utterly, **cast out**, consume, leave for, inherit **-ance, -or**, enjoy, **take possession**, give to possess. *2818* Heir kleronomos, klay-ron-on-eh-o, to be an heir: obtain by inheritance, a possession-inheritance, heirship, a patrimony in the orig. sense of *partitioning* an *inheritor* a possessor;

Rom 8:17 and if we are [His] children, then we are [His] heirs [also]: heirs of God and fellow heirs with Christ [sharing His inheritance with Him]; we must share His suffering if we are to share His glory.

Gal 4:5-7 To purchase the freedom of (to ransom, to redeem, to atone for) those who are subject to the Law, that we might be adopted and have sonship conferred upon us [and be recognized as God's sons]. *6)* And because you [really] are [His] sons, God has sent the Holy Spirit of His Son into our hearts, cry, Abba (Father)! **Father.**

7) **Therefore you are no longer slaves but a son; and if a son, then an heir by the aid of God, through Christ.** *Kleronomos* applies to the heirs of the heavenly Canaan - to hold, have in one's power the act of inheriting an possession. Heirs to a heavenly Canaan. Divine salvation considered both as promised and as already bestowed, is designated an inheritance, so far as man, the heir obtain possession of it.

Definition: 5206 huiothesia from 5207 son and tithemi 5087 to place, adoption: receiving another into the relationship. Son is reserved for the Son of God. Primarily signifies the relationship of offspring to parent and not simply that birth as indicated by *teknon* **5043**. *Huisthesia* places a person in the position of a son. 5207 Huois son, is the quality or character of a son. The expression (proorisias eis huiothesian) **means to appoint before hand to adoption**. Metaphorically: prominent moral characteristics. *huios* refers to those who show maturity acting as sons it gives evidence of the dignity of one relationship and likeness to God's character. The important thing to consider again is when predestination is used it is not **who** the objects of the predestination but **what** they [kings, heirs, sons] are predestined to: which is always to salvation: adoption or glory.

Definition: Prothesis *4286* a putting forth to view or to openly display, a thought or purpose. From (protithemi 4388) before, forth and (tithemi 5087) to place. To propose, to set forth or before the eyes, **design beforehand**. [Ref. Rom 8:28, Eph 1:8-11] *4862* Joint Heir sun, soon; denoting union; with, or together; implying a nearer and closer connection as joint heirs. A joint working cooperation as an **instrument** by, through the virtue of **society** a process of being joined, knitted, framed together through association and companionship, instrumentality, all together.

Mt 5:5 Blessed (happy, joyous, spiritually prosperous-with life-joy and satisfaction in God's favor and salvation, regardless of their outward conditions) are the meek (the mild, patient, longsuffering), for they shall **inherit the earth 1093**!

Definition: 1093 earth ge, ghay; soil, region, world, *terrene*, globe (incl. the occupants of each application):- country, ground.

Normal Works Transformed To Unified Works

Mt 9:38 So pray to the Lord of harvest to force out and thrust laborers into His harvest.

Definition: 3793 ochlos a *vehicle*; a *throng*; a class of people; a **multitudes**, peoples disorganized or unorganized a heathen **nations** usually referring to Israel - the body of Christ all together.

Definition: 4130 fill pletho, play-tho; to "*fill*", influence, supply; fulfil (time). *2986* flow yabal; **to bring forth** from *4130*; flood-tide, **by anal.** a *freshet*:-

flood. *3826* all pamplethei, pam-play-thi; in full multitude, i.e. concertedly or simultaneously - all at once; (*2644*) to *change mutually*, (fig.) *to compound a different*- reconcile.

Rev 21:24, 26; The **nations** shall walk by its light and the rulers and leaders of the earth shall bring into it their glory. *26)* The nations shall bring glory (the splendor and majesty) and the honor of the nations into it.

Definition*: 4128* fullness plethos, play-thas; a *fullness*, a *large number*, throng *populace*:- bundle, company, multitude. *4129* plethuno; to increase - abound, multiply. *4118* **pleistos** plice-tos; the largest number or very large: very great, most, more in quantity or guality, more excellent. *4183* large polus, pol-oos; *much* (in any respect) many, abundant, altogether, plenteous.

Mt 10:5-6; *5)* Jesus sent out these 12, charging them, go nowhere among the Gentiles and don't go into any town of the Samaritans; *6)* But go rather to the **lost sheep of the house of Israel.** Mt 10:7 And as you go preach, saying **the Kingdom of God is at hand**! Mt 22:2, 10; *2)* The kingdom of heaven is like unto a certain king, who gave a wedding banquet for his son *10)* And those **servants** went out on the highways and got together as many as they found, both bad and good, so [the room in which] the **wedding feast** [was held] **was filled with guests**.

Unified Measurement of Work

Ps 105:44 And gave them the lands of the nations [of Canaan], and they reaped the fruits of those peoples' labor. **2 Corinthians 10:15, 16** 15) We do not boast therefore, beyond our proper limit, over other men's labors, but we have the hope and confident expectation that as your faith continues to grow, our field among you may be greatly enlarged, still within the limits of our commission. 16) So that [we may even] preach the Gospel in lands [lying] beyond you, without making a boast of work already done in another [man's] sphere of activity [before we came on the scene].

Definition*! 4883* joined sunarmalogeo, soon-ap-ol-loo-ag-eh-o; to render close-jointed together, organize compactly: be fitly framed (joined) together. 4886 joint sundesmos, soon-des-mos; from *4862* and *1199* ligament (of the body) or shackle, bond, chain, bind; a joint tie uniting principle, band, *control: 4909* co-labourer sunergos, soon-er-gos from *4862* a co-labourer, companion in labor fellow-helper **-labor, -worker**, labourer together with. *4888* exalt sundoxazo to exalt to dignity in company glorify together; refer *4885* to increase, grow up together. *4924* sunoikeo, soon-od-keh-o from *3611*-to occupy a house, reside, (remain, inhabit): to cohabit:- dwell. (*3625*) land, the (terrene part of the) globe:-

earth, world: (*4924*) to reside together as a family:- dwell together. *4929* arrange suntasso arranged jointly, to direct: appoint. (From *5021*) to arrange in an orderly manner, assign to a certain position or lot:- set, determine, appoint, ordain. *4829* partaker summetochos, soom-met-okh-os; (from *3353*) participant, a sharer, an associate:- fellow partaker, partner; *4829* co-participant:- co-partaker, to share and partake jointly.

Christ Glorified through Man's Works

Heb 6:1 Therefore let us go on and get past the elementary stage in the teachings and doctrine of Christ, The Messiah, advancing steadily toward the completeness and perfection laying the foundation of repentance and abandonment of dead works [dead formalism] and of faith to God.

Definition! 5046 teleio goal, purpose, full-grown, of full age opposite to little children or babes in Christ. Reaching the goal set for him by God with each individual differing according to his God given ability, one who has attained his moral end which was intended; that having reached his attainment, **other and higher ends will open up before him in order to have Christ formed in him more and more.** Perfection is not a static state, it's dynamic. 5047 teleiotes -perfection; **stressing the actual accomplishment of the end in view.** Ref. Heb 11:40 Because God had **us** in mind and **had something better and greater in view for us,** so **they** [the heroes and heroines of faith] **should not come to perfection apart from us** [before we could join them]. 5050 teleios **refers to the completeness as an attainment already reached and completed**, also the fulfillment of promises. 5051 teleiosis A completer, perfecter, one who brings something through to the goal so as to win and receive the prize. 5055 teleo To end, complete or accomplish anything, not merely to end it, but to bring it to perfection or to its **destined goal**. Frequently it speaks of fulfilling or answering promises or prayers. When it speaks of definite periods of times to be completed or fulfilled, with the meaning of perfect accomplishment of that **work** whereby the scriptures is fulfilled, not merely to fulfill. In which case telos 5056 means termination with reference to time, the termination of what went before or as a result, consummation. It means the goal reached, the beginning of a new order of things.

Heb 12:2 Looking away [from all that will distract] to Jesus Who is the **Leader and the Beginner or Source** of our faith [giving the first incentive for our belief] and also its **Finisher** [bringing it to maturity and perfection]. He, for the joy [of obtaining the prize] that was set before Him, endured the cross, despising and ignoring the shame, and is now seated at the right hand of the throne of God. [Ref. Rev 1:11]

Heb 2:10 For it was an act worthy [of God] and fitting [to the divine nature] that He, for Whose sake and by Whom all things have their existence, **in bringing many sons into glory**, should make the Pioneer [author, leader, captain] of their salvation perfect [should bring to maturity the human experience necessary to be perfectly equipped for His office as High Priest] through suffering.

Definition! *3648* holokleros From *3650-* **Holo** all, whole, and *2819* **Kleros** a part, share. Whole having all its parts, sound, perfect. Bodily; mental and moral entireness. Related to *5049* **teleios** and **artios** *739* with all its needed parts. That which retains all which was allotted to it in the beginning. **It expresses the perfection before the fall**: Syn. artios 739 sufficient, completely qualified, all the parts of which are complete **what they are supposed to be so that they can reach their destined purpose!**

1Thess 5:23 And may God of Peace Himself sanctify you through and through [separate you from profane things, make you pure and wholly consecrated to God]; and may your spirit and soul and body be preserved sound and complete [and found] blameless at the coming of our Lord Jesus Christ. **Holokleros** is one who has preserved, or who having once lost has now regained his completeness. 2 Tim 3:17 so that the man of God may be completely proficient, well fitted and thoroughly equipped for **every good works**. Gen 1:26 God said, Let us [Father, Son and Holy Spirit] make mankind in Our image, after Our likeness, and let them have complete authority over the fish of the sea, the birds of the air, the [tame] beasts, and over all of the earth, and over everything that creeps upon the earth.

Transform from Men Work to God's Works

Phil 4:17 Not that I seek or am eager for your gift, **but I do seek and am eager for the fruit which increases to your credit** [the harvest of blessing that are accumulating to your account].

Definition! *4851* profit sumpher, soom-fer-o; to bear together, bring forth, collect, to *conduce*, advantage:- be better for, bring together, be expedient (for), be good, be profitable for.

Jn 14:12 Verily, verily, I say unto you, he that believeth on me, the **works** that I do shall he do also; and **greater works** than these shall he do; because I go unto My Father. Mt 25:34 Then the King say to those at his right, come, you blessed of My Father [you favored of God and appointed to eternal salvation], inherit (receive as your own) the kingdom prepared for you from the foundation of the world.

Mt 5:10 Blessed and happy and enviably fortunate and spiritually prosperous (in the state in which the born-again child of God enjoys and finds satisfaction in God's favor and salvation, regardless of his outside conditions) are those who are persecuted for righteousness.

Mt 4:17 From that time Jesus began to preach, crying out, **Repent (change your mind for the better, heartily amend your ways**, with abhorrence of your past sins), for the kingdom of heaven is at hand.

Definition! 3346 transfer metatithemi, met-at-ith-ay-mee; to transfer, transport-exchange, change sides:- carry over, repent, to think differently, transferal (to heaven), to lead over, transfer (direct).

The Freedom of Rest in God's Holy Time Cycles

Eph 1:10 That in the dispensation of the fullness of times he might gather together in **one** all things in Christ both which are in heaven and which are in earth; even to him:

Definition: 346 one anakephalaiomai; a head or sum total. **To gather together again in one**, to **reunite** under one head. 4931 consummation from 4862 and 5055; to complete entirely, to execute, entire completion, consummation of a dispensation: end, finish, fulfill.

Heb 4:9-11 So then, there is still awaiting a full and complete **Sabbath rest reserved** for the [true] people of God; 10) For he who has once **entered [God's] rest** 2663 also has ceased from [the weariness and pain] of human labors, just as **God rested** from those labors peculiarly His own. 11) **Let us therefore be zealous and exert ourselves and strive diligently to enter that rest** [of God, to know and experience it for ourselves], that no one may fall or perish by the same kind of unbelief and disobedience [into which those in the wilderness fell].

Definition: 2663 rest kat-ap-ow-o; to settle down; to colonize or to cause to desist:- cease abode, give rain; reposing: peace and tranquility. **Absence of movement**, refresh by rest.

Jn 4:35 Do you not say, it is still four months until harvest time comes? **Look! I tell you, raise your eyes and observe the fields and see how they are already white for harvesting**. Mt 13:12 For whoever has [spiritual knowledge], to him will more be given and he will be furnished richly so that he will have abundance; but from him who has not, even what he has will be taken away.

Definition: 4920 suniemi; involves the activity of knowing, with immediate knowledge: putting something together and making sense of it. Strictly denotes the collecting together of individual features of an object into a whole.

Mt 5:48 Be ye therefore perfect even as your Father in heaven is perfect. 1 Pe 1:16 Because it is written, Be ye holy; for I am holy.

1 Jn 4:4 Ye are of God, little children, and have overcome them, because greater is He that is in you, than he that is in the world. [1 Jn 3:9]

1 Jn 5:4, 5; For whatsoever is born of God overcomes the world: and this is the victory that overcomes the world, **even our faith**. 5) Who is he that overcomes the world, but he that **believeth** that Jesus is the Son of God.

Eph 1:10, 11 [He planned] for the **maturity of the times** and the **climax of the ages** to **unify all things** and **head them up** and **consummate them in**

Christ, [both] things in heaven and things on the earth. *11)* In Him we also were made [God's] heritage (portion) and we obtained an inheritance; for we had been foreordained (chosen and appointed beforehand) in accordance with His purpose, Who **works** out everything in agreement with the counsel and the design of His [own] will.

PROMISE PHASE 2: WORKS
INTERLUDE: The Divide

Dut 1:2, 3; 2) (It is only eleven days journey from Horeb by the way of Mount Seir to Kadesh-barnea [on Canaan's border; yet Israel took forty years to get beyond it]). 3) And in the fortieth year on the first day of the eleventh. Dut 3:25, 27 I pray You, [will You not just] let me go over and see the good land that is beyond the Jordan, that goodly mountain country [with Hermon and Lebanon]? [Ref. Ps 133:3] 27) Get up to the top of Pisgah and lift up your eyes westward and northward and southward and eastward, and behold it with your eyes, for you shall not go over this Jordan. **Mt.12:25; Every kingdom divided against itself is brought to desolation and every city and house divided against itself shall not stand:**

Here we have the same model of dichotomy, set forth then as it is today changed into many different forms of religious and non religious sects over the course of a long and changing history. Unfortunately, the cause and operation of Satan is still the same to kill, steal, and destroy. It is ironic that Satan main focus was and still is though the fragmented religious organizations and their denominations; as well as the political, military, and specifically the economic system.

Winston Churchill once said that "empires of the future are empires of the mind". Consequently the quality of our empires is based on worldly, symbolic information in our heads. "Garbage in garbage out" points to the premise that the manifested results are always predicated on the quality of the mind that is interpreting the meaning and value of the quality of information based on our frame of reference. In the long term, the results will have social, political and economic impact within our own minds and eventually the empires or democracies that we have established and will build in the free world globally today.

Another cliché: "If you keep doing the same thing, expecting different results you will keep getting the same results that's **insanity**". We hear this quoted quite often, but the truth of the matter is that the insanity continuously increases making the conditions and its results worse. That is a sin which have us as a society in economic despair and lunacy which by the way is another name for Satan.

The historical empires of Satan though the NWO (New World Order) has metamorphosis from **empire to empire Nimrod to Pharaohs of Egypt to Nebuchadnezzar's Babylon, then to Persia, Greece, Rome, Europe, the Soviet Empire and the U.S. of the Americas** are old orders that doesn't give up their power easily. To illustrate briefly from an economic standpoint the government is like a **ticking time bomb** waiting to explode. All we need to do is look in the mire of the antiquated past and the insane, fruitless results of the present and how it has inevitably been passed down in our every day life as an accepted way of life through example and experience. From lifestyle to lifestyle, generations to generations, and unfortunately over centuries throughout history we can look through a panoramic view and take some panoptic snap shots of both the murky past and an even murkier future. That is why any attempt to uproot the injustice against the agents of Lucifer is a no win situation against the chaotic and oppressive debt trap.

In James MacGregor Burns book "Leadership" he is quoted as saying that "all governments in itself is one vast evil". He wrote that Government might change obsolete laws from ancient means and methods in order to address political issues, but it can not of itself generate economic and social liberties for the masses; especially, since the masses of society drives the debt laden system they are enslave to. Although on top of the food chain the capitalist on the same note; is in essence dependent more so on the investor then on the general public who by the way provide the larger percentage of the capital. The investor drives the business market (BM) of the capitalist, but the banking system though the FED **which is a privately owned corporation** regulates, manipulate, and drives all the debt instruments is the glue that seemingly connects the three sectors **(banking, big business, and the general public)** of society together.

Only when there seems to be no choice does this statement "we can't live with it and can't live without it" ring true about a debt ridden life in all three levels. Unfortunately, that is why the negative image and the consequences of **capitalism** are hated by society because of its symbolic alienating implications. However, we still desire and accept its meager contributions and abuses. This describes the repugnant attitude that the majority of the world has toward **capitalism** even before the pre-industrial European era and after America's post industrial revolution in 1790. In retrospect, the first secretary of the treasury Alexander

Hamilton government refunding plan for the new republic was considered by his peers to have "touched the dead corpse of the public credit and debt that it sprung upon it feet" and unfortunately America was build on debt.

When fundamental conflict between two opposing forces is not resolved they fester and cause regression to earlier periods. One example that illustrates this type of regression is when **America broke away from the centralized imperial government of Europe-London, Britain, France, Spain, etc. and their oppressive and diabolical debt system**; and yet, **America** eventually move from becoming a creditor nation to a debtor nation becoming the very government they had escaped from. In America the phobia of debt was given a **schizophrenic** twist just on the fact that this country was reluctantly built on **debt**. **America** eventually followed the inescapable tradition and dependency on the very system of debt and reviled conditions they were fleeing from in Europe. Eventually when the conflict was resolved the complexities and challenges have intensified and tensions transmute into the next stage of synthesis, where a new contradiction begins, and the process starts over again but only at higher levels of tensions. As an example, **politics** regardless of administrations is like a run away juggernaut, being driven by previous financial activities created on all fronts by entrenched erroneous practices inherent to any political system using the debt system. Misplaced blamed is always targeted against any present administration. They have only inherited and replicated the results of previous administrations; which in most cases only farther compounded the negative affects of the underlying cause.

For example the election cycle within the political process of congress is under extreme pressure to balance the budget and pass bills. The **executive** leadership is significantly restricted within shrinking sets of time restraints to respond to progressive financial short falls. These short term responses to long term dilemmas have already been established for them by earlier decision makers. In addition to that, with congress limited time restraints and the repetitive bombardment from long term dilemmas contained within a short term framework, all issues of government will have to be carried over from previous administrations to the next. This process have become so prevalent and inherent to government's short term **political thinking** that the system starts to neglect or cut back government services of the poor and their **entitlement programs** of the working class. And, as a result, when the need to address over bearing crisis **the political process** becomes highly stressed and the characteristic state of backward reasoning become responsive toward effect rather than the cause.

The model again is the same and the trickle down affect within the business arena is also under extreme financial pressures to produce quarterly profits for their investors and if they fail to produce profits the corporations either goes out of business, ridden with scandal they file for bankruptcy. In either case the investors loose and the taxpayer always absorb the costs. Massive corporate layoffs, depletion of retirement and pension funds seems to be the primary solution to company's financial short fall. The debt system is having such a negative affect on the smaller business economy in ways that the investors in the upper class of society along with corporations and the **political system** is being ripped apart. Therefore, a big disconnect is forming between the political leadership, big business, and eventually on down to its hard working class of the consumer. Government debt, business debt, and consumer debt is increasingly carried over year after year. There seems to be no fiscal accountability; because the deterioration of the world financial system is continually being broken apart the trickle down effect, which has started collapsing and deteriorating the very fabric of society and its people.

Like a *tsunami* the **debt system** recedes back into the underwater earthquake waiting for the point of closure. The underwater earthquake creates a highly pressurized suction stop: (a large intake of vacuumed air and water pressure) that is sucked into the ocean floor of the earthquake and than gushed out as a powerful tidal wave violently moving miles inland. This example resemble what happens to a kingdom divided when the concentration of all the variables of debt are magnified within a implosive vacuum, that will instantaneously be released from its temporary state of pregnancy; and in time, it will become the inherent and progressive patterns of experience to those locked in the **closed debt system**. Eventually it will burst inwardly marking the beginning of momentum which has accelerations independent of any imposing barriers and impeding boundaries.

That is why in 2005 we have witness catastrophes after catastrophes: The **tsunami** in Sri Lanka, the devastation of Katrina and society wonder where the resources (funds) are and why the contributions that have been collected over the decades aren't there to meet the devastation and the needs of the people. We should be able to see the parallels across the board and the trickle down affect from government bail out programs for top executives and the businesses they run under the U.S. bankruptcy protection program, the saving and loan fiasco created by(HUD, Freddy Mac, Fannie Mae, The Treasury, the FED, etc.), worker's pension plan shortages and the mismanagement of pools of billions of dollars of retirement funding at the expense of retirees, share holders and their worthless stocks, while all of the cost is transferred over with the tax payers holding the bill. There is nothing new under the sun the system has been broken down and can no longer respond efficiently or effectively to any crisis for positive long term solutions. In our vanity there is a sense of emptiness in society and a worthlessness that is always associated within Satan's debt base system.

When we look at the catastrophes (**Katri**na) throughout the world we start to witness the inadequacies to respond as it relates to the negligence of the government, (home land security, FEMA, and the Red Cross) in handling the devastation suffered by Louisiana's citizens we look with dismay and wonder how could this happen to a whole state in the United States. Again, there is nothing new under the sun and the un-regenerated mind set of the political leadership who has become so restricted that the demagogue have suppressed quality information and impedes most needed reform from the top down limiting choice and responsiveness to catastrophes. Such confusion and complexities ruin great plans when financing have been abused and lacking. Such dogma and schisms is inherent to a restricted mind set. It is also inherited by those few leaders who benefit from the system prior and wish to maintain their power and status quo at all cost at the expense and negligence of the majority.

The past abuse and negligence is evident when the need to reform the **third rail issues** (tax reform, social security reform, health care reform, and retirement-pension reform, and the results of war) eventually requires serious overhauling and repair. In fact, any quick solution is usually destined for failure over a short period of time. The mere thought of sweeping reforms is creating electrifying shock waves of fear and concerns throughout the political arena, society, and the monetary system especially during the two terms of **George W. Bush administration**. A similar scenario existed during the reconstruction period after the civil war

These **third rail issues** are factors that have heated up over time and like a **pressure cooker** is reaching a boiling point that demands serious attention. The unified forces are accelerated at such a dazzling pace not because of what any one administration does or doesn't do. But the precedence of what previous administrations over the centuries were forced to do themselves by increasing spending, raise taxes, the inability to stop the continuous increase of the deficit; corporate scandals, steady increase in short term interest rates, gasoline prices skyrocketing, hurricane the **wars** prior to the **Iraqi war**, hurricane Katrina, and high unemployment rates.

When these factors are exacerbated by international warfare, the judiciary responsibility of the government domestic affairs becomes neglected especially when federal cut spending and the United State national debt is steadily increasing will only worsen with greater intensity down the road. Forcing the international bankers of the world: Japan, China, United kingdoms, Russia, and Caribbean banking center, just to name a few to default on holdings of trillions of dollars of this country's nation debt.

These are all contributing factors that are imploding the entire economic system. <u>It's the national and international bankers, insurance, and investments companies that make up the three money pools and control the world financial system instead of Congress who had render control of the monetary system through the Fed Reserve Act of 1913 opening the door to manipulation of the financial market</u>. This is nothing new; it has been the American way since the U.S. left Europe. The reforms run the gamut from tax, health care, welfare, and social security reforms, which were issues that needed to be addressed and overhauled decades ago.

Historical Start of Usury

Fernand Braudel in his work "The wheels of commerce" p565 quoted Giulio Mandick "The 17th century by which a long term loan was made through the system of exchange and re-exchange, the practice of circulating a bill of exchange for a very long period increasing the repayment amount from year to year. When the practice was condemned as pure usury long representations was made and finally persuaded Urban the V111 to recognize it as legitimate on September 27, 1631." When we look back in time and to the present, the powerful elite of Europe have always superimposed its financial strangle hold on any nations that had rendered control to the financial establishments of the international bankers dating as far back as the 14th century, even to the present when America render control in 1913 to the federal government. In further retrospect looking back in time to see a similar pattern emerging again where the image of Islam had even foreshadowed that of Europe; which was past on by the Muslim economy and piggy backed on the economy of the Middle East (not on to the world of Greece and Rome) had a greater respectability that related to commercial life.

That is why, any attempt to revolutionize change in the way wealth is created and one immediately collides with all the entrenched power of the NWO (new world order) nationally or globally from the political, corporate, or religious arena. Their power arose from prior wealth systems that had change in appearance only but not in substance. It's these types of political distractions and the conflicts within the monetary system that is designed to trigger the present power shake ups that have been spreading across the globe today specifically the war in the Middle East which will be discuss later.

Short Term Debt Eliminated Mike Milken

If as difficult as it may be, we must go back to the short term ideology of financing the masses other than long term debt and interest carry over; in order to bring balance to the debt structure and offsetting its overwhelming affects to long term interest. In addition to that, implementing a long term strategy will reduce long term loans and credit while at the same time maximizing wealth creation for the larger populations and not the second and third tier corporation locked mainstream financial establishment eventually prohibiting him and junk bond from being used in the investment industry.

But up until that point, Mike Milken example reveals one important dimension of creating wealth quickly by basically establishing **short term** debt then reducing that debt and converting it into liquid cash or real money outside of the status quo. These massive sums of liquid short term capital can then be injected into the economy not as perpetual debt creation through long term lending but reproducing and perpetuating liquidity and raising the economic value and the equity. Thereby, eliminating the dependency on the ideology of long term debt creation which prohibits government officials from serving the social/health programs that are being cut because of a reduction in federal spending as the cut back affect trickles down throughout society. **It is true then that a kingdom, city or house divided against itself can not stand.** Interestingly enough, those attached to the world debt system, although not initially apparent will feel the ripple effects eventually. However, the cause of debt is more confined between the government and the business sector, but its affects over time will inevitably be reflected in the consumer sector as the pressure builds.

So taking a look at the historical parallels of modern day events we can see similar patterns. Unfortunately **MICHEAL MILKEN** had experienced this first hand but that's what happened during the junk bond era of the 1980s. To illustrate the enormous power and untapped beauty within the imploding chaos in government and business let us take a brief panoramic view in modern history of **Michael Milken** "the junk bond king". The concentration of Milken activities was to trim bureaucratic fat in the corporate world and possible government.

The purpose of his story is to show the validity behind the ideology of **short term** debt; how it can be managed and have a profound affect on long term debt within its **closed system;** especially outside of it as it relates to the masses.

However, **short term** debt like in the past will eventually get swallowed up in a cyclonical downward spiral of the long term debt trap. The elimination of it came since the focus was and still is to perpetuate the long term enslavement to it not to reduce it dependency of it. America have inherited debt phobia from the British and the Europeans and it was the instrument of risk upon which the pioneering spirit had been built.

Whoever attempt to bring balance to the lopsided world financial debt system might break the financial isolation imposed upon the business market temporarily; although, in the long run, it will be to no avail. The results of these impositions are to maintain the status quo of the establishment or gatekeeper of the business world regardless of the benefit. Forcing them to hoard a large percentage or at least what seem to be large percentages of a small pie that is deteriorating. But in actuality it is a very small percentage when viewed only from within the closed debt-based economic, monetary, and investment systems. **Milken** seen the strong ardent desire for assess into the debt and rating system by corporations and their investors was like a rushing river that had been dammed up.

An enormous pressure built up behind the dam but when it burst the enormous power broke the psychological lock of the debt system and released an ocean of capital into 95% of the lower tier companies that was outside of the establishment grading system and considered junk companies. Because the debased junk bonds had changed the structure of corporate America in less than a decade. At first, the debased junk bond benefited the establishment and the Wall Street titans; however, their choice of debauch, bankrupt bonds – (although that was exactly what it was suppose to do give them at least greater fluidity within a much larger market) gave them more control long term than junk bond did short term; the old order could not see outside of their retrograding paradigm. Therefore the establishment main rating agencies Moody and Standard & Poor could not encompassed both anomalies of a broader concept. Embracing the inclusion of a larger pool of corporations could only benefit business a hundred fold and transcend beyond the retrograde of their **inevitable anathema**.

The negative impact throughout any transitional phrases will have a gradual and predictive decline in lifestyles for future generations after the retirement of the baby boomers. The repercussions that will be felt during this massive drain by retirees will also produce a real financial void against the actual financial void which already pre-existed. As we get closer to the anal of the transitional phrase, the gradual depletion of national savings and the **accumulated reserves** of both the social security system and the retirement program are the short term and long term effects of recession and depression. Recessions are cousins of depression that has short-term erosive affects within the transitional phrase can reduce economic activity which are reflective in depreciated decline in profits, sales, production and unemployment but depressions only precipitate the exacerbations in between the transitional splits that it actually created.

Although the erosive affects devalued the savings initially, it will be the compound economic pressure of the international currency wars by the international lender who holds control over the U.S. debt and rather to choose not to buy anymore debt. The probable scenario that have always loom is that all of our savings could be transposed into the international credit market, just as it has been predicted and is being planned by the government.

Normally, in most instances by the time a response has been provoked the allegations against the seemingly irrational extremes of this transverse dichotomy, has already deepened its influence upon the economy. Although this is the big picture, the underlying distractions, diminishes the allegation that's proliferating throughout the news media reporting more of the symptoms than the actual cause of the problem. This is the reason for the great fears and anxieties of today's events in society both here and abroad which are but small episodes of distraction designed to divert attention from the grander scheme of commercialization. That's why Jesus didn't deal with the world system understanding the hideous destructive spirit behind its myriad of causes, effects and agencies. From the domestic or international front the results will always weight heavy upon any government leadership and the political, social or religious institutions that wishes to engage in it.

Unless of course you're a financier where money is king which drives commerce; who normally profit during these transitional periods of depression. It is important to understand that at the height of any given transitional phrase a transposition shift have given national or international bankers control of what used to be a tangible liability.

When the transposition occurs and it will, it will have an **inverse affect** upon society; whereby the psychological dependency on our entitlements and social security and retirement programs will shift to a dependency; more so, to the credit markets of investments and the corresponding relationship to it. This regressive detachment which holds an opposite viewpoint of what society is accustom to but must become accustom to. It is a fact that the present economic disparities will become more disproportionate making it very difficult to distinguish between the various regressive detachments.

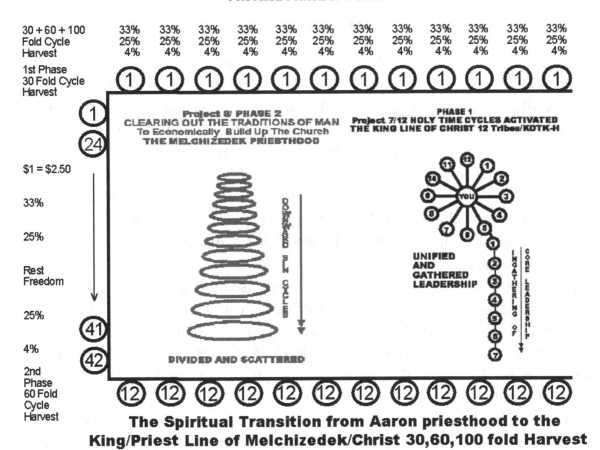

| 30 + 60 + 100 Fold Cycle Harvest | 33% 25% 4% | 33% 25% 4% | 33% 25% 4% | 33% 25% 4% | 33% 25% 4% | 33% 25% 4% | 33% 25% 4% | 33% 25% 4% | 33% 25% 4% | 33% 25% 4% | 33% 25% 4% | 33% 25% 4% |

The Spiritual Transition from Aaron priesthood to the King/Priest Line of Melchizedek/Christ 30,60,100 fold Harvest THE HERITAGE OF JACOB

Figure 7

FIGURE 7 GRAPH EXPLANATION

Figure 7 is the transitional graph for *figure 5* denoting the priesthood that's divided and scattered. In order for *figure 5* to become *figure 6*; whereby, the **king's office** is put above the priest office becoming one and then; consequently, receiving Adonai greater promises and blessings (indicated in the diagram as the 30, 60, 100 fold harvest or business cycles that has been transposed for today into points and compound percentages 4%, 25%, 33%, etc.) which operates for and within the **king's office** and outside of the 10% tithe system of the Moses/Aaron priesthood. For this to happen, the priesthood must submit to the prominent office of the **king line of Christ- his kingdom structure.** But until this prophetic decree is obeyed, the transition of the **heritage of Jacob** in *Figure 7* will not be transferred throughout the 3 promise phases.

Figure 7 shows the divide between **circle 24** and 41. Circle 24 is the priesthood/church and is indicated by the 12 circles with 1's in them and represented graphically by project 8/phase 2 and *figure 5*. **Circle 41** is the **king line of Christ/priest line of Melchizedek,** which offsets and breaks the downward sin cycles of the operation of the antichrist, and circle 41 is indicated by the 12 horizontal circles with the 12's in them represented by phase 1 graph. When *figure 5* do transition into *figure 7*, it is not just transitioning into *figure 7* and closing the gap; but as a result, the divine power comes when the integration process happens simultaneously into *figures 6* and accelerated instantly by *figure 9*. All this potential activity of the operations of the spirit happens when *figure 5* and 7 becomes *figure 6*.

PREDESTINATION OF SALVATION
Transition Point Spiritual Preparation

Mt 2:27 The Sabbath was made for man, and not man for the Sabbath. Therefore the Son of man is also Lord of the Sabbath. *John 4: 35) Say ye not, there are yet four (4) months and then cometh the harvest? Behold, I say unto you, lift up your eyes, and look on the fields. For the fields are already white for harvest.*

Is 58:13, 14 *If you do not tramp upon the Sabbath by doing **your** business on My holy day, but call the Sabbath a **spiritual** delight, the holy day of the Lord, honorable, and honor Him and it, not going your own way or doing your own business nor seeking your own pleasure or speaking with your own [idle] words, **Then shall thou delight thyself in the Lord; and I will cause*** *thee to ride upon the high places of the earth, and feed you with the heritage [promised for you] of Jacob your father for the mouth of the Lord has spoken.*

Mal 3:2-4; *2)* But who can endure His coming? And who can stand when He appears? ***3)*** *For He is like a **refiner's fire** and like fullers (launderer's soap); He will sit as a refiner and **purifier of silver**, and He will **purify the priests and the sons of Levi, and refine them like gold and silver, that they may offer to the Lord offerings in righteousness**. **4) Then** will the **offering** of Judah and Jerusalem be pleasing to the Lord as in the days of old and as in ancient years*.

Heb 11:4 *[Prompted], activated by faith Abel brought God a **better and more accepted sacrifice than Cain**, because of which it was testified to him that he was righteous [that he was upright and in right standing with God], and God bore witness by accepting and acknowledging his gifts. And though he died, yet [through the incident] he is still speaking.*

Heb 12:24 And to Jesus, the mediator (go-between) of a new covenant and to the sprinkled blood which speaks [of mercy and redemption] a better and nobler and more gracious message than the blood of Abel [blood of vengeance].

Transition from Levitical to Judah

John 3:29, 30; 29)*He who has the bride is the bridegroom; but the groomsman who stands by and listens to him rejoices greatly and heartily on account of the bridegroom's voice. 30) This then is my pleasure and joy, and it is now complete. He must increase, but I must grow lesser.* [Ref. Is 9:7; Zech 12:7, 8] Heb 6:20 **Where Jesus has entered in for us in advance, a forerunner having become a High Priest forever after the order of Melshizedek**.

Mt 9:37, 38; 37) *Then He said to His disciples, the harvest truly is plentiful, but the laborers are few*. 38)*Therefore pray the Lord of the harvest to send out laborers into His harvest*. Ps 105:**44 *And gave them the lands of the nations and inherited or reaped the fruits of those people's labor*. Jn 4:38** *I sent you to reap that for which you have not labored; others have labored, and you have entered into their labors*.

Is 40:3 The voice of him that crieth in the wilderness, prepare ye the way of the Lord, make straight in the desert a highway for our God**.**

Jn 3:30, 31; 30)**He, Christ must increase, but I must decrease**. He who comes from above (heaven) is [far] above all [others]; he who comes from the earth belongs to the earth, [his words are from an earthly standpoint].

31) He who comes from heaven is [far] above all others [far superior to all others in prominence and in excellence]. Mt 11:10, 11; This is the one of whom

90

it is written, behold, I send **My** messenger ahead of you, who shall make ready **your** way before **you**. 11)Truly I tell you, among those born of woman there has not risen anyone greater than John the Baptist; **yet He who is least in the kingdom of heaven is greater than he**.

Mt 11:28-30; 28) Come to me, all you who *labor* and are *heavy-laden* and *overburdened,* and I will cause you to *rest.* [I will ease and relieve and refresh your souls.] 29) Take My yoke upon you and **learn of me**, for I am gentle [meek] and humble [lowly] in heart, and you will find rest [relief, and ease and refreshment and recreation and blessed quiet] for you souls. 30) For My yoke is wholesome [useful, good, not harsh, hard, sharp, or pressing, but comfortable, gracious, and pleasant], and My *burden* is light and easy to be borne. Heb 9:11, 24 But [when that appointed time came] when Christ **the Messiah** appeared as high priest of better **promises** that have come and are to come. By a greater and more perfect tabernacle, not made with hands, that is to say, not of this **building** or material creation. For Christ **the Messiah** has not entered into a sanctuary made with hands, only a copy and pattern and type of the true one, but [He has entered] into heaven itself, **now to appear in the [very] presence of God on our behalf**. Lev 25:14 *And if you sell anything to your neighbors or buy from your neighbor, you shall not wrong one another. Lk 19:13 Calling ten of his own bond servants, he gave them ten ninas [each equal to about one hundred days wages or nearly twenty dollars] and said buy and sell, [do business] while I go and then return*.

I Cor 10:24 Let no one then seek his own good and advantage and profit, but [rather] each one of the other [let him seek the welfare of his neighbor].

Ps 112:3 Wealth and riches shall be in his house: and his righteousness endureth forever.

Ex 1:7; *But the descendants of Israel were fruitful and increased abundantly; they multiplied and grew exceedingly strong; and the land was full of them*. 2 Chr 29:34-36 But the priests were too few and could not skin all the burnt offerings, so until the other priest sanctified themselves, their Levite kinsmen helped them until the work was done, for the Levites were more upright in heart than the priests in sanctifying themselves. Also the burnt offerings were in abundance, with the fat of the peace offerings, and the drink offering for every burnt offering. So the service of the Lord's house was set in order, Thus Hezekiah rejoiced, and all the people, because of what God had prepared for the people, for it was done suddenly.

Ex 19:5, 6 Now if you will obey My voice of truth and keep My covenant, **then** you shall be **My own peculiar possession and treasure** from among and above all peoples; for all the earth is Mine. <u>And you shall be to Me a **Kingdom of Priests**, a holy nation</u> [consecrated, set apart to the worship of God]. These are the words you shall speak to the Israelites.

Dut 32:9, 10; **9)** *<u>For the Lord's portion or apportionment is His people; Jacob became the Eternal's share [Jacob was the allotment for Him to hold]. 10) He found him in a desert land, and in the waste howling void of the wilderness: He kept circling around him, He scanned him [penetratingly], He kept him as the apple of His eye</u>*.

Mt 10:34-36, 38, 40) *34)* Do not think that I come to bring peace upon earth; <u>I have not come to bring peace but a sword</u>. *35)* For I have come to part asunder a man from his father, and a daughter from her mother, and a newly married wife from her mother-in-law. *36)* And a man's foes shall be of his own household. *38)* **And he who does not take up his cross and follow Me** [cleave steadfastly to Me, conforming wholly to My example in living and, if need be, in dying also] **is not worthy of Me.** *40)* He who receives and welcomes and accepts Me, and he that receives Me receives and welcomes and accepts Him Who sent Me.

Termination & Transition: A New Priesthood

Heb 7:11 Now if perfection [a perfect fellowship between God and the worshipper] had been attainable by the Levitical priesthood - for under it the people were given the law - why was it further necessary that there should arise another and a different kind of **Priest, one after the order of Melchizedek,** rather than one appointed after the order and rank of Aaron?

Heb 7:12 For the priesthood being changed, there is made a necessity a change also in the law.

Transformation & Reorganization: Spiritual Repentance

Heb 7:13 For the One of Whom these things are said belonged [not to the priestly line] but to another tribe, no member of which has officiated at the altar. [Ref. Is 9:6, Lk 2:11, Jn 3:16] Heb 7:14 For it is obvious that our Lord sprang from the **tribe of Judah**, and Moses mentioned nothing about priests in connection with that tribe [Ref. 1Jn 2:20-24] Heb 7:18 So a previous physical regulation and command is cancelled because of its weakness and ineffectiveness and uselessness.

Mt 15:3, 5, 6, 8, 9, 13, 14; 3) But he answered the Scribes & Pharisees saying, why do you also transgress the commandments of God by your traditions [handed down to you by your forefathers]? 5) *But you say, if anyone tells his father or mother what you would have gained from me [that is, the money and whatever I have that might be used for helping you] is already dedicated as a gift to God, then he is exempt and no longer under obligation to honor and help his father & mother. 6) So for the sake of your **tradition** [the ruler handed down by your forefathers], you have set aside the Word of God [depriving it of force and authority and making it of none effect]. 8) These people draw near Me with their mouths and honor Me with their lips, but their hearts hold off and are far away from me. Mt 15:9 Uselessly do they worship Me, for they teach as doctrine the commands of men; [Mt 15:13] He answered, every plant which My heavenly Father has not planted will be torn up by the roots; [Mt 15:14] Let them alone and disregard them; they are blind guides and teachers. And if a blind man leads a blind man, both will fall in a ditch.*

PROMISE PHASE 2: WORKS
INTERLUDE: The International Affects of War

Jesus warned kingdom leaders about the current negative events about wars of wars and the rumors of wars and not to be troubled, nor be concerned about it because all these things must happen. Ironically, and in retrospect, we should thank God that the church leadership of his time could see only murder and consequently, the divine plan to kill Jesus. Was Jesus killed because he went against conforming to the traditions and cultural customs of the world? Yes, in stark contrast one could emphatically agree! However, there's a greater awareness that runs antithetically parallel to Christ purpose and its relationship to the rulers and church leadership that must be identified and brought to light, before we can proceed farther in understanding with clarity the humor behind the chaos

To illustrate briefly, today the world is witnessing progressive changes along all fronts. Especially during the post 9/11 where the first time **Iraqi** elections surrounded by global terrorism internationally (from the **Middle East, Russia, Europe, London, Britain**) and all the pros and cons of media press along with their gallop polls are proliferating confusion, doubt, fears and concerns that are associated with wars. What I found intriguing is the numbing condition that persists in the majority of society here and abroad, where people seem insensitive towards the spread of freedom abroad for others. That only a select few can enjoy the so call freedoms that are enjoyed in America and throughout other parts of the world.

But more importantly, by spreading democracy globally terrorism eventually loses it grip on a controlled people who never experienced freedom are now being given some hope of freedom with a price to be paid. America before it was free had to fight a **civil war** in Europe. It was the colonial's freedom from Europe rule to start America. A civil war that freed blacks from slavery, the Berlin wall demolished, Jews freed from Hitler's control who was once hated outcasts in Europe. These historic events became possible because of fearless leadership. As usual, over time history will reveal the impact and their after effects in some form or another.

Let's start briefly with some of the most recent and revile events the **Iraq war** and President George W. Bush's vision and commitment to win the war and eventually the peace. James Mac Gregor Burns book "Leadership" quoted two statements of Levin in 1917 as it relates to revolutionary leadership: "Never play with an uprising, but once it has begun, be firm in the knowledge that you have to carry it through to the end….once the uprising has begun, one must act with the utmost decisiveness….and go over to the offensive….One must strive daily for at least small victories…in order to maintain at all costs moral superiority" and "to elevate the goals of humankind, to achieve high moral purpose, such as freedom, to realize major intended change, leaders must thrust themselves in the most intractable processes and structures of history and ultimately master them".

Historically, this is nothing new Christ warns us in Mt.24:6 "And ye shall hear of wars and rumors of wars: see that ye be not troubled: <u>for all these things must come to pass,</u> but the end is not yet". [Ref. Rev.9:17-19; 11:7-10] There is nothing new under the sun and wars has been an inherent part of man nature since the being of human existence. The focus unfortunately today, is on the war in Iraq which most of the international community by large was against and non-supportive of it. Over sixty eight percent of the United States wasn't just against President Bush choice to go to war but also the need to overhaul the social security system along with reforming the healthcare systems that previous administrations did not address. President George W. Bush, Jr. won, amidst all the seething hostility, the hard fought campaign in 2004 by the Democrats to assure President Bush did not get re-elected to a second term.

The results of 9/11 and the **Iraq war** preceding it has reverberated an awakening of sorts in America and around the globe with beheadings and suicide bombings, The resilient attacks by the insurgents, kidnappings murders and killings, the high unemployment rate as well as corporate scandal and massive job layoff, unfavorable economic climax, the deficit in the health care industry where millions are without health care insurance. The depletion of the social security system is by far the biggest asset of most American households along with the bankrupted pension system, and the list of disparities goes on; bankruptcy is at an all time high, pay day loan lenders saw an increase of in business in 1993 of 200 outlets to 27,000 plus outlets in 2004 and the industry is operating at 500 billion dollars.

These atrocities only indicate the high tolerance of pain and suffering the consumers and corporations have been willing to endure instead of changing. People rather stay dependent on these types of entitlement programs and other social welfare programs for generations before they are forced to change and move out of their comfort zones. We have over centuries and decades been willing to zigzag from one failed debt-base investment system to another. In some impoverished sectors of society have stayed unemployed and dependant on some type of subsidized program that are being cut back and the tax burden is continuously being shifted to the middle and upper class: whereby the quality of their lifestyle is becoming more difficult to maintain and as a result the middle class are becoming impoverished. How low can society go! How much will our culture endure?

The seemingly new economic crises and the strident structures of one scandal after another have cause for; at least for the short-term, some critical amalgamated reforms: Remember why did the 401k pension plan come into existence? Because of the 500 billion dollar savings and loan crisis that is suppose to address the long-term dilemma but fell short. It seems to have the same negative short term results. The scheme just been repackaged to supposedly address what was not address previously, with the basic, erroneous personal account premises and principles that produce the negative results still in place. Again, that's insanity. Let me remind you that "there is nothing new under the sun and ignorance is bliss". You are not insane and you will not be stupefied or surprised any longer when you hear, watch, read or experience these perturbations. This generation of young adults and teenagers are already targeted to inherit and participate in the same system that is laden with the same conditions and live with the same devalued, binding depreciating results, and so the insanity continues on.

This is the inheritance that the thieves had stolen, plundered and pilfer aged for their own uncontrollable passions, inordinate selfishness, vanity and hypocrisy. The **wealth produce** from this type of money isn't money at all, and this juggling of monies and the book-keeping and accounting system, along with the taxation system have become so confusing, that it seemed not only complicated but diabolical. The **wealth created** has always been illusory wealth, a lot of money with little effect and very seldom returning to the larger sectors of society its people or the church leadership for that matter as profits. It is this condition that describes the repugnant attitude the majority of the world has toward capitalism before the pre-industrial European era (by choice) and post industrial revolution by default. Today, we still find ourselves as the majority of society eighty percent are still disconnected from participating in the profit structure of the economic system while; at the same time, being in bondage to it.

The International Backlash of War

Kingdom Leaders must take heed to the great wisdom of Christ Jesus when he warned us about the current negative events about wars of war and the rumors of wars and not to be troubled about it because all these things must happen. Ironically, and in retrospect, we should thank God that the church leadership of his time could see only murder and consequently, the divine plan to kill Jesus. Was Jesus killed because he went against the traditions and cultural customs of that time? Yes, in stark contrast one could emphatically agree! However, there's a greater awareness that runs antithetically parallel to Christ purpose and its relationship to the rulers and church leadership that must be identified and brought to light, before we can proceed farther in understanding with clarity the humor behind the chaos. Historically, this is nothing new Christ warns us in Mt.24:6 *"And ye shall hear of **wars and rumors of wars**: see that ye be not troubled: <u>for all these things must come to pass, but the end is not yet</u>"*. [Ref. Rev.9:17-19;

11:7-10] There is nothing new under the sun. **Wars** have always been an inherent part of the human experience since the beginning of human existence.

The normal forces within Satan's **closed loop system** get worse over time; **because it** pit one government against another. Eventually the merging of these forces are **split apart** releasing whatever pent up energy there is and transform it into a radical political and economic system. The forces released by the democratic process that was thrust upon say an autocratic regime such as Islamic fascism, socialism, communistic forms of government can prevail in the democratic process and become fused into diverse and unstable radical elements. When these types of factors (revenge, hatred, tensions, animosities, conflicts, hostilities, frictions and fears of all sorts) reach such breaking points and start slamming upon one another within governments the results resembles the principles of an atomic and nuclear reaction.

James Mac Gregor Burns book "Leadership" quoted Levin in 1917 as it relates to revolutionary leadership "Never play with an uprising, but once it has begun, be firm in the knowledge that you have to carry it through to the end…. once the uprising has begun, one must act with the utmost decisiveness….and go over to the offensive….One must strive daily for at least small victories…in order to maintain at all costs moral superiority." And "to elevate the goals of humankind, to achieve high moral purpose, such as freedom, to realize major intended change, leaders must thrust themselves in the most intractable processes and structures of history and ultimately master them".

To illustrate briefly, today the world is witnessing progressive changes along all fronts. Especially during the post 9/11 where Iraq for the first time held democratic elections while surrounded by global terrorism and corruptions internationally (**from the Middle East, Korea, Russia, Europe, London, Britain**) and all the pros and cons of media press along with their gallop polls are proliferating confusion, doubt, fears and concerns that are normally associated with wars. What I found intriguing is the numbing condition that persists in the majority of society here and abroad, where people seem insensitive towards the spread of **freedom** abroad for others. That only a select few can enjoy the so call **freedoms** that are enjoyed in America and throughout other parts of the free world. **We have forgotten however, that America was once probably seen as rebels against the European community and as a result outcast.**

But more importantly, by spreading democracy globally terrorism eventually, so it is believed, may lose its grip on a controlled people who never experienced **freedom** are now being given some hope of freedom with a price to be paid. Just as those before us had to fight there was many other wars, conflicts and riots fought as well. The colonial's **freedom** from Europe rule to start America, African Americans freedom from slavery and white supremacy, the Berlin wall demolished, Jews freed from Hitler's control who was once hated outcasts in Europe. These historic events became possible because of fearless leadership. As usual, over time history will reveal the impact and their after effects in some other form or another when another President will have to deal with the consequences of the previous administrations.

To prove the point that whoever or whatever attempts are made to bring balance and justice or maybe even freedom to a system locked within a **closed loop system** rather it is though the financial debt system, the political process, or the democratic process might be able to temporarily break the psychological isolation but its impact unfortunately won't be felt for decades down the road. Why? Because the spread of democracy globally sometime though **war,** will naturally bring about self destruction then reconstruction in order to build the structures for the new establishment in order which to support the civilization and its culture. However, any attempt for revolutionary change in the way wealth is created and one immediately collides with all the entrenched power of the (new world order both nationally or globally. Their power arose from prior wealth systems that had change in appearance only but not substance will fight to the end to maintain the status quo. It's these types of political distractions and the conflicts within the monetary system that is designed to trigger the present power shake ups that have been spreading across the globe today specifically in the **Middle East.**

Let's start briefly with some of the most recent events of President George W. Bush's decision to go war, and the stubborn vision and commitment to protect the people of the United States. By winning the **war** on terrorism and eventually winning the peace. The focus unfortunately today is on the war in Iraq which most of the international community by large was against and non-supportive of it. The United States leadership and the society as a whole are split on seemingly all issues and policies both domestically and internationally. The results of 9/11 and the Iraqi war following it created great **divides** among most of America's alliances to go to **war** against Iraq; who by the way, over history have fought **wars** against one another just to become allies afterwards. Such alliances are a result of unsolved matters left over from previous **wars** are all interwoven by crisscrossing relations, so that any one **factor** of past **wars** can have serious consequential impact in the future. Here is the irony behind all of this that no one could have known or predicted except God himself.

The latest development came in January 2006 when the least likely terrorist group **Hamas** won a landslide victory over **Fatah**. Who national policy is the destruction of **Israel** which America has supported. These small but significant victories show the unpredictability of the democratic process to produce greater instabilities in the **Middle East territories**. In addition, the foreign peace policy is now jeopardized. Any attempts by the U.S. to impose sanctions on **Hamas has a ripple affect that is highly volatile** in other newly emerging terrorist nations (Iraq, Iran, Syria, Beirut, Pakistan, Baghdad, and their fashions)which is a form of hypocrisy on the part of America if the people of Palestine chose the better of two evils though the democratic process. This will create the opportunity for outside support from neighboring terrorist states (**Egypt, Lebanon, Iran, Syria, Palestine**), who also won independence though the free elections of democracy.

Not to mention, other major players in the **Middle East** who are looking to increase a greater presence for control in the oil rich territories of the Persian gulf by China, or U.S.S.R. with billions already invested in that region. More so today, the national debt continues to expand as it where, to spread and dump the world debt system into the underdeveloped decolonized nations though the World Central Banking System. We have witness the liberation of the **Middle East** and the development of a constitution by election in Dec. 2005. However, the Middle East is a gold mine for extending the debt system throughout that region.

The larger sectors of society haven't differentiate these historical examples of transitions reveal that their detachment must take place over time as America attempts to become more competitive by expanding its unregulated monetary policy internationally, are being force to grapple with the reciprocal affects of U.S. foreign economic relationships with its foreign allies that is more economically stimulating as globalization positioning heats up in America. This reciprocal preference towards foreign policy has unfortunately an inverse relationship in the handling of the domestic affairs associated with national security, immigration, unemployment and domestic federal cuts in social services, etc. which appears to have taken a back seat in the inattentive eyes of society for foreign policy while military spending increases. The larger aspects of America's economic disparities are magnified between domestic and foreign policy and its inverse affects. We can see the inverse affects in the globalization into America is having upon their opposing viewpoint, but more so now in the U.S. since American asset has been up for sell.

Domestic Policy

Hydrogen Bomb Affect

All of Satan's financial schemes are like the **hydrogen bomb**. The principle of fusion behind the hydrogen bomb will give you some resemblance of the destructive nature of Satan's mindset. The greater the **dichotomy of Satan's split** the greater the **implosion** of profits (trillions of dollars) into the domestic market of his world debt system and the greater its infusion or explosion of Satan's debt-credit instruments (long term: investments-domestic and globally, long term 40 year mortgages and their accompanying insurances, 5 to 7 years auto loans with interest, direct and in-direct credit card interest, internet banking fees, service fees, etc.) into the entire world markets creating greater disparities across all fronts domestically and globally.

There is no turning back, because the extension of globalization by America is penetrating deeper into the Middle East territories from **Iraq** then and now into **Iran** and **Palistan**. This is characteristic of the non-stopping ratcheting effect of the **implosion** and **infusion** of capitalism and the democratization of it in the Middle East. Although the transmutation of the super symbolic technology and the credit-debt system has already been implemented nationally, the permeating activity of hoarding will gradually continue to intensify globally on all domestic fronts through almost every business transactions over time and eventually over the internet once its all is integrated; this is the characteristic of the debt-credit systems of the world system. Satan's system resembles that of a **hydrogen or atomic bomb** the most destructive weapon ever devised in the twentieth century. The normal results of Satan's economic system and financial schemes are indicative of two opposing reaction acting upon one another similar to that of the atomic and hydrogen bomb. The smaller atomic bomb is used internally to ignite the more explosive **hydrogen bomb**, although there is individual reaction of destruction in each. The basic principle behind the atomic bomb is **fission** the process of splitting apart a single nucleus. However, **fusion** is the process behind the hydrogen bomb where the collision of neutrons is shot at the nucleus of an unstable isotope of hydrogen under extremely high temperatures releasing enormous quantities of pent-up energy. Creating the most destructive thermonuclear weapons ever devised in the twentieth century, and by comparison Satan's economic debt system resembles this thermonuclear process of the **hydrogen or atomic bomb.** The economy heats up-overheat with too much debt in the system

According to the Department of Treasury sources that CIFIUS (The Committee on Foreign Investments in the United States) who reported that since 1994, ninety two American assets have been purchased by foreign governments. The most recent attempt was by DPW-Dubai Ports World of United Arab Emirates bid to take over operations at six U.S. Ports a $6.8 billion deal. The deal was defeated on Capital Hill 3/9/06, however, the fall out could have reciprocal repercussions that will widened the economic divide and intensify the disparities of the domestic policies looked at as a liability. While at the same time slowly receding back into isolationism, which will mostly affect national domestic policy especially if most needed foreign investment capital recedes for the American market.

The disparities within the world debt system illustrate the divisive dichotomy the world debt system has when the reciprocal relationships are disrupted. Foreign nations have extensive holdings in America's liabilities, which have been developing at an accelerating rate and since America have expanded capitalism globally, it is now being taught a thing or two about capitalism by foreigners-terrorist organization included. Foreign countries are aggressively and extensively investing in American assets through finance, insurance and banking in America. This backlash stems from the U.S. government lackadaisical oversight and as a result, America is losing its positions as the premier global competitor.

Despite recurrent anxiety attacks and paralyzing fears in the case of economic insecurity that America is being taken over by foreigners extends far beyond terrorism far beyond the war. The long standing tendency of America reaction to globalization has been to escape isolation especially now, since the U.S. economy has been increasingly intertwined with the rest of the international community; specifically the Middle East nations who are the latest foreigners with several holdings of American assets in America.

Here again the distress and fear in domestic and international dichotomy is oscillating at such a high rate that public opinion and its perception is deliberately withdrawing which is a form of isolationism within the changing climate that is maximizing the world debt system.

Like a **tsunami** the debt system receded back into the underwater earthquake waiting for the point of closure. The underwater earthquake creates a highly pressurized suction stop: (a large intake of vacuumed air and water pressure) that is sucked into the ocean floor of the earthquake and than gushed out as a powerful tidal wave that violently moves miles inland. This example resemble what happens to a kingdom divided when the concentration of all the variables of debt are magnified within a false vacuum, that will instantaneously be released from its temporary state of pregnancy; and in time, which have been the inherent and progressive patterns of experience to those locked in the **closed debt system**. Eventually it will burst inwardly marking the beginning of momentum which has accelerations independent of any imposing barriers and impeding boundaries.

Here's an explosive example of how the **dichotomy** behind all wars and the irreversible forces which drives it to a destructive end. Wars and their consequences can be compared to the most destructive thermonuclear weapon devise in the twentieth century, the hydrogen bomb. Where the smaller atomic bomb is used internally to ignite the more explosive **hydrogen bomb** has clearly altered diplomatic relations in foreign policies, and the economic collapse, failures, and pressures in supporting a war. Within this explosive state are constant simultaneous activities of contractions or an expansion that have multiple compressed affects within them that literally crushes the atomic nucleus and split apart those parts. This is the basic principle behind the atomic bomb called *fission* which is the process of splitting apart a single nucleus creating an implosion or abrupt inward burst.

On the other hand, *fusion* is the process behind the hydrogen bomb and the general principle is the collision between neutrons and the nucleus of unstable isotopes of hydrogen under extremely high temperatures; releasing enormous quantities of pent-up energy which are fused together with other diverse binding elements. The after affects of this 1st blast creates the intake of infused intermingled radioactive mixtures and atomic nuclear chemical elements from the 2nd blast creating a compound after affect of radioactive ash fallout; that affects is more devastating later than the initial effect itself. The synthesis of the diffusion process can not be identified by introspective analysis or its long term effects and in comparison this is how Satan's system works.

Simply put, the previous **splitting** by the United States in the underdeveloped autocratic nations of the Middle East has diffused an agitated blend of complex sentiments at such accelerated speeds; that the underlying characteristics of its transformations or phase transitions are seldom recognizable but reactionary by our present society. The intensity and tensions are escalating dramatically and reaching breaking points which burst into civil wars throughout the regions of the Middle East that its effects are being felt worldwide. However, it's not the end of a war that leaders should be concern about but the weakened financial state of America and the repercussions of nuclear build up and the consequences that normally effect future policies diplomatically with other nations as a result of war.

Ignorance about this splitting factor creates extreme uncertainty, fear, and anxiety within a people during times of **war.** Strong resistance to war along with the threat of going to war is a result of intense antagonism and pronounced divisions between cultures and nations. **Wars** is an extremely emotional state; involving love ones and is displeasing to society because of the beheadings, kidnapping, suicide bombings, kamikaze, submarine attacks, torture, murders and killings.

But when you couple these factors with the of economic devastation domestically you eventually end up with financial shortfalls will force transformations in America's domestic affairs such as tax reform, high unemployment rate, as well as corporate scandal and massive job layoff, outsourcing jobs to foreign countries, unfavorable economic climax, the continued approval and increase in federal spending negatively impact skyrocketing federal deficits in the government that's deteriorating the health care industry where millions are without health care insurance. The depletion of the **social security** system and the bankrupted pension system is by far the biggest asset of most American households and again the list of disparities goes on. Bankruptcy has reached such an all time high that congress had to legislate limitations against the increasing corporate and personal bankruptcy rate. These are abused issues that have lacked fiduciary responsibility as a result of weak, partisan political leadership. They will find the pressure extremely challenging and difficult to address resulting in a regressive state of pessimism and criticism. However, it takes strong, unified leadership to move forward with solid policies, solutions backed by strong action.

The international landscape is rapidly changing also and the U.S. international policy must change accordingly; which is now dictating powerful unpredictable implications in handling our own domestic affairs. There is a delicate balance between freedom and the various global clashes of instability in a world of **autocracy from totalitarian, dictatorial, monarchy, imperialism, feudalism and now terrorism**; not to mention the subdivisions that have split into various splinter regime organizations. The **Cold War** could be considered the turning point for the post war superpowers (U.S., Europe, China and Russia) and their diminishing control and influence over the new international landscape that has independently transformed pluralistically and simultaneously though the free elections of democracy.

This is becoming apparent during a time when nuclear programs in these newly emerging constitutional democracies are increasingly expanding and evolving with greater intensity; seemingly, outside of the influence of the superpowers. However, it was the **American Revolution** that set the precedence for third world countries seeking their own nationalistic independence from **Europe** to follow suit; when America spun off from Europe in the early 18th century and won its independents in 1776.

In the first quarter of the 21st century the world specifically the U.S. are passing again though the disheartening cycles of despair while the hope for the democratic road map to peace have taken a sudden horrible shift toward the tyrannical and dictatorial direction in the **Islamic republic**.

Although the difference are apparent, it appears that the ideology of freedom behind the constitutional statements in the Declaration of Independence **"one nation under God, government of the people, for the people and by the people, equality and inalienable rights, justice and liberty for all"** seem to be a contradictory ideology and are repudiated in the middle east by extremist and have created an implosive regression; though which the political conflicts of the **Iraq war** have triggered an even greater explosion of pent up repression expressed as global violence and civil war throughout the third world countries among the Muslim communities.

Even in today dramatic turn of events, we see repeated cycles of involution; whereby the backlash from the revolution is having powerful implications for our own nation and on many failed occasions, this has become a seeming embarrassment not only for the United States, but for the U.S. constitution that is looked upon as a viable model for constitutional makers everywhere. Unfortunately, this is the characteristic dichotomy in its evolutionary process of shifting to lower states of severe intensity resulting in backward reasoning.

But over time and out of history enemies have became allies developing into diplomatic coalitions such as the United Nations; but it stands as a fact, for whatever reason, that although they were once autocratic they eventually become allies for freedom. This happened only when strong leaders, regardless of the failures or set backs, must demonstrate against insurmountable odds the God given authority to fight a good fight for the liberties and freedom for others which in most cases indirectly tied to their freedom in some way that was probably being slowly threatened. However, if we don't stand for freedom who will? Eventually, God will have to.

PROMISE PHASE 3: TIME

HARVESTING THE SPIRITUAL MOMENTS OF NOW

Ecclesiastes 3: 15 That which hath been is now; and that which is to be hath already been; and God requires that which is past.

Within the "**now**" is that spiritual place when time and action seems to stand still; although it remains operative outside of now. However, even before and after this place, time and action will have been trying to become "**now**" where rest and peace resides. In other words, God's time even "now" is omnipresent and it is here where wisdom lives. Wisdom is hidden in (**Olam**) and revelation is hidden in the eternity of the eons called Olam. (Olam) is the time or axis that all other times evolve around. At the same time, Olam compasses all spiritual activities while simultaneously embellished with all the fullness of the times. Some of these characteristics are the times of restitutions and the times of restorations and the times of refreshing. ***These are predetermined times that cycles though pre-appointed seasons throughout the circuit or the landscapes of the earth. Even now, the predetermined times lay in abeyance for the opportunity to manifest kingdom economics though those "kingdom leaders" who see and claim the opportunities for dominion within God's kingdom.*** Olam is not affected by the vicissitudes of the "dispensational" periods of history. It is at this timeless point that once the interpretation has been internalized, kingdom leaders can freely enact their relationship to eternity. Most of this sounds foreign to us because "predetermined time" according to the kingdom of God operates outside of our natural consciousness of time which is either projected in the future cycles of the debt system or remembered from our actions based on past accumulated labors.

Chronos are successive moments of linear activities at sequential time periods. They are also separate manifestations of activities at various intervals; while at the same time the kairos can be at rest, fixed and hidden within the horizontal dimension of the chronos. It is at these intervals (fixed points, moments in time); that the qualities and quanties of times within our time period, the quality within men life-time, from generation to generation [vertically] and to a thousand generations [horizontally] in which all the divine times of God are complete within itself. It was between these intervals (harvests) which over time released the appropriate action (all promised blessings) at that pre-appointed time of manifestations (all seasons cycles). The consummation of every possible pre-appointed time (kairos) is encompassed in the chronos.

It is pregnant and stored up within all of the various kairos; eth (right time), Hara (**hours**) Yom (**one day phenomena**), the sabbatical (**days, weeks, years**) and the jubilee just to name a few. All of the time periods were sequential as well as random events within the holy time cycles, which is indicative of the seasons that once passed though the inheritance (the land) of the multitudes and blessed God's covenant people. The oneness of God was manifested more so then; than at the present time today in our society. Basically, because the divine structure of the tribes were foreknown to be united then than now; therefore, we have become scattered, and disconnected from our inheritance. God's people then were connected to their inheritance (the land) also; thereby, unifying them with the economy of the kingdom of God. In short, the old Jerusalem is the past. It has commingled with and is now encompassed within the New Jerusalem of the future. This holistic oneness of the New Jerusalem offers greater qualitative improvements in men than the old Jerusalem could ever before offer outside of men today. But we as kingdom leaders must recognize that better promises exist today!

The seasonal harvest of the past is transformed today into the geometrical aspect of time compounding. The transitional results from the agricultural era to the information age will be quite munificent when connected with the symmetrical dynamics of compound unity among the multitudes represented as space. These copulative affects of unity and the holy time cycles upon the multitudes create a copious manifestation of the many sided covenant promises and integrated with the combinations of the overcoming blessings will be a unique financial phenomenon for kingdom leaders positioned in today's super symbolic era. Once the kingdom principles of scriptures are reinterpreted, then a new reconstruction of our old paradigm can than be converted and upgraded to the vanishing point of the times and seasons regulated by the impulses of God. It will be those kingdom leaders who understand and adapt to the moves of God that will play a transforming role in applying the principles of kingdom economics, and the powerful impact it application will have upon the marketplace today. This phenomenon has not been experienced yet, but has been proclaimed and decreed by Christ.

This is the New Jerusalem (The kingdom of heaven) that is from above and is free from the restraints and constraints of a one dimensional concept that's normally associated with the material realm of land and earth. The New Jerusalem that's free requires kings to demonstrate dominion over the limitations of the earth. *Kingdom leaders must mentally shift their understanding that realistically associates with the geometrical relationship of time and faith as they pertain to prophecy based on Gods revelation to man.* In addition to that, the symmetrical scope concerning unifying and integrating the multitudes back into the economy of the kingdom as one complete circuit in the market place is the holistic view we must grasp concerning God's plan of redemption for his people. The consummation or the **fullness of the times** represents the holy time cycles of the Lord of harvest and the operation of the spirit is the epitome of the prescient statement: "***prove me now herewith, said the Lord of hosts, if I will not open you the windows of heaven and pour you out a blessing that there shall not be room enough to receive it***". Kingdom leaders must learn to receive these blessings simultaneously, in order to receive **God's holy time cycles** we must be taught again to think in cycles of holy times which is kingdom economics.

This momentous statement reveals the alpha and omega of Christ. So since His beginning and His ending is in eternity then he can be manifested completely and perfectly in our hearts. Until the ordinary become extra ordinary, our ordinary experiences between the last times, won't chronologically start a new beginning. It continues on that same old linear path unaffected. That's why you can ask someone what's happening and the response normally is "nothing"! That's why between these intervals of times the quality of life for the multitudes has become stagnate and therefore we are humans constantly becoming instead of humans being-perfect now! Recall the decree of Christ, "***Be ye therefore perfect***". In other words, before every starting point there is a beginning and the end of time is not the last. Therefore, the quality of our lives will be better than our last best as long as we live in the present now. As kingdom leaders the next second should be better than the last second when Christ glory is magnified in them. This will occur when we as kings begin to envision the appearing of Christ's revelations as our own, which are locked up in time; therefore, qualitatively renewing our ordinary experiences making our life experiences **extraordinary**.

Recognizing that revelations are locked up in time and time is laid up in Christ, as kingdom leaders we must come to realize more that Christ's timelessness is perfect and complete within itself right now. With that being the case, we as kings must **expect a better present** and see past promises and its future blessings as a now reality in our present situations today. There is no more sowing and reaping for the mature (perfect) it Christ because Christ said, "***He always reaped where He did not sow". He is our beginning and our ending and His father is the same yesterday, today and forever***.

In Acts 3:21, we understand that heaven (New Jerusalem) has given temporary accommodation to Christ Jesus, which is his temporary residence in the eternal. Meantime, His appearing are contained in the prophetic revelations and the revelations are compressed in time and consequently, time is laid up in Christ. Until we understand the fullness of the revelations in Christ, His illustrious coming will not shine its light or instructions upon kingdom leaders; for that reason, prophecies will remain locked up. <u>In our unfulfilled past and a **proleptic anticipation** of future promises and blessings will leave countless voids outside of the present now state of eternity</u>.

These voids or separation points have always typified immense opportunities to bring together the prophetic decree from the past to the future combined with the **proleptic anticipation of God's promises** from the future to the present manifested into our (kingdom leaders) present now experiences only though a timeless relationship with Christ. Because we have not recognized this great fact, we as beneficiaries to the promises according to God's holy time cycles have become totally dependent on the world debt system. The world system which is diametrically opposed to kingdom economics and is inherent to any debt based system where the reward (illusionary wealth) is based on future payout (either after retirement or upon death) rather than present wealth.

God's times (eternal) are fill full of all these times (chronos) at the same time. It may seem counter intuitive that a fixed ending point (perfect or complete) can have an ongoing action or condition. **Gunther Bornkamm** in his work "Jesus of Nazareth" (New York: Harper and Row 1960) p.72 shed light when he states "The end comes from the beginning, the fruit from the seed, the harvest from the sowing...thus our task is to understand the present, in which the coming event already finds its beginning" Mark 4: 3-8. But these progressive and perfect events that are ongoing do not imply that it will never end, but that it is just fulfilled and that any void perhaps, eventually would be fulfilled continuously. It simply means that the void or separation persisted for a notable period of time until such time the erroneous conditions is corrected and ended, than the endless repetition of events can be realized in a positive sense.

Here's another example of **closing the circles** (generations) and filling up the intervals through a simple, but powerful plan to step into the next phase of salvation as heirs, whereby kingdom leaders could be instantly perfected. When we intuitively understand the economic impact of the 12 stones (the gateways or bridges to our soul opens up and deposit all the heritage of Christ) and identify our value according to God's infinite attributes which **fills up** our inheritance (parallel plains, the tesseract of cubes, the cosmos of people and space, or worlds

108

in relations to time) simultaneously. The matured in Christ are in fact that inheritance of God. This simple but powerful process of unification increases the number of dimensions of space and that is combine with time ascends into even higher dimensions of unity within us until all the grace of each promise becomes unified into even **higher dimensions of acceleration and integration**. Through the integrated **operations of the spirit** this type of wealth distribution is specifically designed to drop down to the lower sectors of the invisible economy in the earth (cosmos).

Unfortunately, it is impossible to visualize the magnitude of this type of wealth generation while still trapped in the normal 1 dimensional thinking within the world's debt system that is intuitively and firmly embedded in our brains.

The most essential attribute of three dimensional thinking is having the mental capacity to comprehensively move and shift within the three coordinate positions of all three dimensions simultaneously. However, for these and other reasons this is completing the circle of perfection and is the apex of kingdom leadership. Those who learn to live in the present instead of the past or future will experience greater freedoms in all areas of life. Recognizing not just the inclusiveness and completeness of our kingdom, but that Christ had already established the works (distribution of the blessings) that had already been performed through Christ. It is the mental shift of the kings from the **vertical dimension** to allow the operations of the spirit to take on geometrical proportion between the minds, souls and hearts of kingdom leaders. This is the (faith) works of kings who wisely discerns not only how to apply the chronos (pre-appointed times) to the **horizontal dimension**; but also, allow the works of the spirit to connect with the myriad points of connections between these minds, souls and hearts as only the holy spirit can.

The horizontal dimension is the seat of dominion for kings and the final frontier for kingdom leaders to enact the establishment of the heavenly city upon its inhabitants; namely, those heirs who've claimed their right and authority to become citizens. The horizontal dimension is available to kings to transfer what they themselves had unveiled though revelation which again is **linear**. For we hold the key that opens the horizontal dimension which is the doorway to the soul of man. It is only when the soul of man is engaged into the mind of the spirit that is, the operation of the spirit though the vertical window pouring out into and laying to our hearts the proleptic anticipation of the prophetic promises; and as a result, the actions of the will, affections, passions and emotions of the human spirit are greatly intensified and magnified.

This is the distinguishing mark of kingdom leadership. Those who come to realized their spiritual authority as priest, overcoming things concerning heaven. In addition to that, and perhaps, far more important, is not just governing the revelations of the mysteries or even fulfilling prophecies; but as kings in God's kingdom we're to exercise dominion as heavenly citizens according to kingdom rules here on earth. Who remember the move of God, His counsel, His instructions and His ways? Who will diligently and seriously explore new dimensions in God though the bible and the Holy Spirit? When kingdom leaders reinterpret the scriptures and have their minds reconfigured and their souls converted and their hearts rent; than; as a result, our minds, our souls and our hearts will be upgraded and lifted up to wisdom's gate of the holy city.

Metaphorically speaking – this dimension of wisdom that upgrades and uplifts is the result of entering into wisdom's gates. All the hidden riches of the secret places even the dark riches are stored in her seven pillars which are built upon the foundations of the kingdom of God. The treasuries of the house of God even the special treasures are already filled up in all of the stored cities; while, at the same time, the heavens and the earth have treasures gathered together and heaped up in their storehouses. The overflow of the presses and the vats are congealed in the depths (hearts of the people) and pressed down in the heart of the sea (men) filling the vessels of our hearts with her (wisdom) the most treasured possessions.

Along the eternal time line of the aions space and time are wrap into one unified moment. To appreciate the enormous simplicity of our <u>accelerated inheritance</u> we must visualize the multidimensional unification of Christ heritage. In order to develop the capacity for **higher dimensions** of timeless freedom we must refer to the first part of the Isaiah 9:6 which represent the Cross-(death, resurrection and ascension).

Closing the gap of the past and future and bringing it into the present dispensation today is a simultaneous action of fulfillment; whereby the decree is fulfilled and the promised prophecy of Mt. 19:28 is manifested. Through a structural plan of implementation, kingdom leaders who wish to bring honor and glory to Christ through our success can now enact with sovereignty some resemblance of His government or kingdom rule (dispensation) on earth now not tomorrow through us for himself.

It is this connected integration that bring kingdom leaders into the fullness of His times (the joining of two ages, generations, life-times, or time periods) where the greater plan of salvation for humanity has distinct phases which are consummated in Christ's glory as our demonstration of his blessing. It's these distinct phases (ending of one interval while, at the same time beginning to fill another) that present the opportune times for Christ to magnify the maturity of all the acceptable times (kairos) as one in the earth. In actuality, it presently resembles a continuous process or infinite straight line of filling the voids without any voids or separating points. This unique demonstration brings forth the imminent manifestations of what is meant for God to "Bless our blessing and multiply our multiplying".

That in all of this it has already been manifested in the spirit, more so then than now. In fact, this process will continue to close the gaps in our lives being made whole or two halves into one truth; that being two in one in Christ. (***The kingships and priesthood though Christ for us has became as one, but also our kingship though Christ has also, even now multiplies into twelve and exponentially into144,000 and eventually nations and so on.***)

The psychological lock of most people in general is based solely on our present conditions in reference to our past experiences. All of our decisions should not be isolated on conditions and circumstances where the premise is erroneous and our experiences and sphere are limited based on our own understanding. The disruption of the world was an event which had formed a great dividing time line in the dispensation of the ages, and that only God understand the events that have transpired in the past; as well as those events that will be fulfilled in the future. The world of man have only a limited capacity to the indefinite and concealed duration of the hidden part, but when reunited with the mystery of the kingdom the dividing lines of the successive ages of history are brought together and closed, in that the end becomes the beginning.

The world of man is reunited again back to God. So the fullness of God's purpose can fill up the inhabitants of the earth with his promises. It is here, where the fullness of the times is made apparent to the world. This denotes the indefinite and concealed duration where the fullness of the times are laid in the foundations of eternity. It is now when God reveals mercies of mercies, blessings, and honor and multiplied promises.

Only God understand the end as well as the beginning where he had already laid and hidden his divine purpose, concerning the Remnant, and their hidden promises and blessings. This denotes that within the hidden eons of the ages, God has already shrunk all the times within this indefinite time span, a present moment; whereby kingdom leaders can know and prepare according to his will and purpose. Since God is the totality of all events he knows each event within their totality; it is here and now that God fuses together the collection of the ages, to present a phenomenon. However, when one steps out of human time into eternal time of the kingdom an immediate awareness of eternity is gleamed. It's at this moment that the acceleration upon our consciousness will have simultaneous effects independent of the moment or incident involved. In other words when the complete and perfect comes; the incomplete and imperfect will vanish and be superceded and made available to me by a faith that is assured in God's revelation to me. This divinely implanted principle that is connected to my faith is a **bridge** from which the power of his spirit sought to find occasion for expressing his guidance and protection for me.

3 Personal Life Testimonies

At this point, I'd like to share three short testimonies of moments that I believe was a **bridge** for the operations of the Holy Spirit to find expression; not through the inner subjectivity of my consciousness, but rather independent of it. But more importantly; during these phenomenal events, I was amazed at the involuntary presence of the Holy Spirit within my moments of spiritual awakenings and crises. It seemed to have superseded any conditions or circumstances that I was experiencing at that time by bringing sanity and restoration back to any insane situations that we may experience in life.

The first incident was the day before and the day after my recovery from alcohol and drug abuse. But what lead me up to this was the fact that I was single, no kids, working two jobs, and going to school and felt I was on my way up the latter of success until that day I had my taxes done and was dismayed at the amount of my tax return. So much so that the void in my life had instantly turned into feelings of despair and disgruntlements; and it was at that point I could remember thinking that it was time for me to loosen up and have some fun in life. I didn't realize the impact those words would have in my life and a few week later a long time friend I haven't heard from in a while called to invite me to a private party he was having which introduced me to sex, drugs and money. It was about the month between August and September of nineteen eighty nine when I had reached rock bottom during that final weekly binge over approximately four years; whereby, there were a point of introspection and recognition that my life was out of control as I was sitting down on my couch. It was at that moment in my apartment that it literally looked like I was in a place of hell. It was constantly full of people coming and going who always bought some bodies back with them, running around naked in and out of the thickest smog of smoke I have ever been in; other than the thickest fog that I've ever driven in which I will save for in the second story. I was totally exhausted from the heat, sweat, sex, and drugs as I sat their speechless with the driest parched throat I have ever experienced. I was bankrupted financially, physically, mentally, and spiritually.

My life of descent flashed in front of me at that point and I sought help at a treatment center for a month. The next day I heard a man who looked like Moses to me sharing his story about his alcoholism and drug abuse and afterwards he grabbed my head and said son you're going to make it and for the first time in my life I believed. It was two weeks into the month when my brother who I have not seen in about seven years came to visit me on a Sunday, and this mine you came after the hold unit for whatever reason came against me psychologically to attack my recovery and I retreated to my room to reflect and feel a sleep.

I was awakened by the taps of his umbrella on my shoulder and when I turned around to look I could not believe the joy and happiness of seeing his face; but what was more astonishing then that, I seen something else in him that I had never seen in him before. During that short visit he started talking to me about being a king in God's kingdom and that I was a son of a king and that the king was Christ, the kings of kings and Lord over my life. I had no idea of what he was talking about but it sounded so good to me at the time. Two weeks later he came back to pick me up and that whole evening until the next morning we talked bible which reminded me of the past bible teaching that I had totally forgotten about.

All this was so refreshing to me that I crave to have this thing that he had and he invited me to receive Christ as Lord and Savior of my life. A peace beyond my understanding came over me along with tears of joy pouring out of my eyes that I had never experienced before; but what was to follow was indescribable except that after opening my eyes life inside my eyes literally seemed like heaven. It was in that same apartment that I experienced both hell and heaven and a renewed awakening toward the future.

The second story deals with the guidance of the spirit. While driving alone; to the state of Maryland for a business conference by way of the Pennsylvania turnpike, I found myself engulf in one of the most beautiful, but yet, the worst weather conditions I had ever experienced or driven in. A turnpike is different than a regular highway in that the exits could be several miles apart before you get to the next city because of the mountains.

It was during day and the winter season had just dumped several inches of snow mixed with rain and sleet throughout the state. Night fall came and there was construction going on which reduced the turnpike from 4 lanes to two lanes with concrete barricades on both sides preventing any exit onto the shoulder in case of an emergency. In addition to that I had entered another storm of sleet, rain and thick fog.

Then I realized that my wiper blades had not been wiping the slush from the wind shield away quick enough and a sheet of ice started to develop on the windshield. As I reached to increase the speed of the heater blower, I realized that it was only blowing at minimum capacity. So much so, that the only view of the road I had to look though was between the steering wheel and the small area right above where the heater vent was located. The area of view was so small that I could only focus on looking at the dashes on the road in order to see where I was driving on the road. The focus was so intense that I could not turn to the left or to the right to assess what was going on around me. To make matter worse, the fog was so thick I could not see any vehicles ahead of me or trucks to the left side of me, although I could hear them as they passed by.

Eventually, the only viewing area that I had to see out of was frozen over and there I was instantly blind, and it was at that point when the Holy Spirit spoke with a still soft voice and said turn your head to the right and look at the barricade. Immediately my focus shifted on staying as close to the barricade as I can without moving to far away from it that would interfere with the traffic to my left; which of course could have caused a serious accident. And as I was driving with my head turned to the right focused on the barricade it suddenly vanished, leaving me totally bewildered as to what to do next. It was at this point where I was forced to just exercise faith and pull over, not knowing what I was pulling over into so I did.

After gathering my senses, I realized that my alternator had gone bad which had caused this situation from the beginning. I than got out of the car to assess where I had pulled over to and recognized that I was in the tangent or further most corner of a large trucking shoulder with the front of the car inches from the edge of what appeared to be a deep ditch or gully; which I couldn't tell how deep because of the thick fog. But as I was returning to get back into the car to backup a massive truck flew by and startled me so; because I realized immediately, how close the tail end of my car was to the lane of the on coming traffic; that any vehicle could have knocked the car over into the ditch; but worse still, I could not back up to move out of that predicament. It seem I didn't have a snowball chance in Hades of getting out of this dilemma; because all I wanted to do was get out of the cold into what I thought was a warm car but I was afraid of getting in the car for fear of being knock over the edge with it.

After waiting outside in the cold for some body to come to my rescue; eventually, the cold won over my fear and I scrapped the ice off the windshield and I just got in my car backup onto the turnpike, and headed down the road. It was after midnight when I was finally able to exit the turnpike. I came across two gentlemen who gave me directions to a two hour short cut into Maryland. I was so cold that I was forced to move on down the road totally forgetting that my alternator wasn't working. I was totally thankful and amazed at what my Lord had just brought me though, that the car stopped and coasted right in front of the hotel where a parking spot was waiting.

This third story involved one of protection though an accident I had on my job at the United States Postal Service when the first section of my **left index finger** was accidentally torn off when the glove I was wearing got caught and pulled into the moving mechanism during a simple equipment inspection on my job. In most cases; without even thinking about it, one would have been expected to go into trauma and panic as a natural physical response. However, to my amazement I didn't, but instead an immediate sense of peace came over me right before I briefly looked at the torn off finger and quickly threw my arm behind my back. My mind seemed to have denied the reality that my finger was cut off. In addition to that, I felt no traumatic pain in my arm at all after the ordeal. After all of the commotion of going to the medical unit, waiting to be transported to the hospital, and eventually surgery it was between 1-1/ 2 to 2 hours and still I didn't feel any pain up to that point prior to the nurse rolling in the tip of my finger. It was than when I seen my finger that the pain shot up throughout my arm and the rest was history.

I shared these stories to illustrate the spirit behind them and how the spirit when understood economically could impact the economic aspects of our lives as well. The rest of the book will reveal to the reader the spirit behind kingdom economics. So get ready for an awesome journey through God's Word and the Spirit of God where the Word of God empowered by the Spirit of God becomes a living force in our lives. All these experience over time have revealed one thing to me, that one day or moment with the Lord is like a thousand years or vise versa a thousand years can be as one day or moments in God's time; where as human time and our experiences outside of it, will always lag behind or move to far ahead of God's time. I have come to realize that in an insane situation God could restore us back to sanity instantly.

When one step out of human time into the eternal time of the spirit an immediate awareness of acceleration will start to become evident, bringing about the **activation of the Holy** Spirit. Meaning that when all of God's pre-appointed times; which encompasses his blessings, guidance, or counsel they can simultaneously be manifested in the lives of those who are aware enough to receive them, especially from an economical stand point. It is very difficult to imagine; but when the integration process occurs time will shrink to explosive speeds mentally; whereby we can start to see the elimination of the sequential time and recurrent sense associated with debt in our lives.

When kingdom leaders the remnant seed begin to understand these hidden times the results will be exponential and accelerate the process of integration throughout the lives of kingdom leaders who are the remnant seed. They will immediately become reconnected to the divine administration of grace engaging them into the all encompassing circuit of God's holy time cycles and dispersed throughout the structure of Christ remnant seed filling us up with the promises and blessings indicative of the fullness of the day of the Lord.

This is the process of reconciliation and it closes the gap of separation, which is the turning point when ones conversion is made and the sin of the debt cycles of the world system is blotted out and closed. The closing of the separation gap will produce such an accelerated integration of his people throughout the foundation and the structure of the remnant seed that a single duplication or feed back process will bring about higher ends of maturity and greater restoration of our promises and blessings. Whereby, our blessing is blessed and our multiplying is multiplied. These glimpses of eternity produces such feed back that it accelerate the acceleration process of his holy time cycles simultaneously in the lives of the kingdom leadership.

INTERRELATIONS OF UNITY, WORKS & TIMES

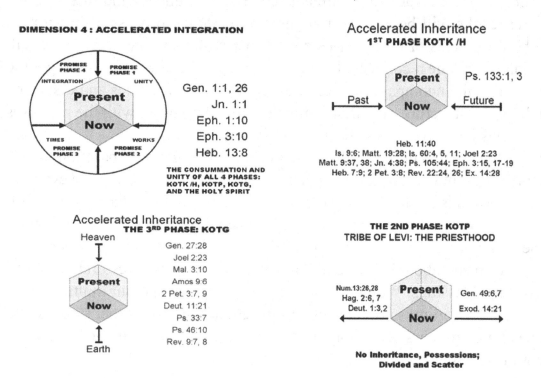

Figure 8

FIGURE 8 GRAPH EXPLANATION

These 3 aspects of the *present now isometric* cube graphs in *figure 8* are designed to help the reader establish a comprehensive framework that nurtures the present now 3 dimensional mindset that is directional in scope. You will find that the 3 phases of the *present now* graphs in *figure 3 & 8* are combinations of other graphs that will biblically help the reader create the mental foundation that supports this 3D thought process, in addition to focusing that mentality toward kingdom economics. This process produces a strong sense of anticipation and omnipresence of God's promises and closely associated within his seasons and the dimension of pre-appointed times that are translated into business cycles for today.

There is one very important fact concerning the **circle 42.** Since Jesus didn't have any kids, **circle 42** had to be the 42nd seed unto **Christ**, with respect to **circle 41** and the 12 disciples, must be the last and only present now generation;

therefore, the **KOTG** is the largest and greatest aspect of the kingdom, which could be bought into the fold of **circle 41** the generation of Christ at an unimaginable rate of acceleration. The dimension of magnification throughout all 3 levels of the **KOTK-H, KOTG AND KOTP** is **the present now activity** of divine grace is like electricity arching between **circle 41** and **circle 42.** This happens when the **acceleration of unity** is intensified by the integration of all 4 phases in *figure 1.* This is all happening in **circle 42** as the **entire kingdom foundation** is raised indicated by the 12 flatten circles (holy time cycles) expanding wider from bottom to top as the KOTG structures made up of 10K's x 12 ascends from **circle 42** and flows into **circle 41** in *figure 9.* This **divine activity of integration** both vertically and horizontally is ultimately consummated in *figure 1* as the foundational structures are developed and elevated economically by the **acceleration process** of the holy time cycles. This is the great harvest of different spiritual qualities (indicated by the jewels within the flattened circles) that the matured kingdom leaders believers and non-believers are made up of as shown in *figure 9.*

Divine Dimensions of God's Time Periods
Characteristics of the KOTG: The Cube

Definition: *5769* Olam o-lawm from *5956* *concealed,* i.e. the <u>***vanishing point;***</u> <u>time out of mind</u> (past or future), i.e. (<u>practically</u>) *eternity; always,* (for, [n-]) ever (lasting, -more, of old), <u>perpetual at any time</u>, beginning of the world, without end, compare. *5331* netsach nay-tsakh; from *5329;* a *goal to glitter* from afar, to be eminent; also to *be permanent:-* excel, overseer, set forward. The bright object at a distant traveled towards; (fig.) splendor, or (subj.) truthfulness, or (obj.) confidence. But usually (adv.) continually (i.e. to the most distant point in view): perpetual, strength, victory. To the vanishing point of a lifetime, (compare with generation).The basic meaning of olam is "the most distant times and has a broad range between the remotest time and perpetuity (from the viewpoint of the seer). Eternity should not and can not be just limited to some future state of ambiguity. But when human time is replaced with God's times in the present now, then we have a better understanding of his will in our lives.

Eccl 3:11 He has made everything beautiful in its time. <u>Also He has put eternity in</u> <u>men's hearts and minds</u> [a divinely implanted sense of a **purpose working through the ages** which nothing under the sun but God can satisfy], yet so no men cannot find out what God has done from the beginning to the end.

118

The KJV translates olam as "world", ***without beginning, without end***, and ever continuing. "Olam" indicate an indefinite continuance into the very near future but is not confined to the future. The God of Abraham was not touched by the **vicissitudes of time**. "Olam" can describe a *short period of only 3 three days though it must have seemed like eternity to Jonah*, Jon 2:6 *I went down to the **bottoms of the mountains** that rise from off the ocean floor.* I was locked out of life and imprisoned in the land of death - tay. The Sept. generally translates olam by aion *165*, and often translated to "world". *165* Aion - ahee-ohn from *104 - duration; "ever"*, *earnestly*: refer to an age or time, in contrast to kosmos (*2889*), which refer to people and space. *1)* Both in the sing. or plur. it signifies **eternity** whether past or future to come, the next life; since the beginning of the world. Time in its duration, that is, constant, **abiding** used when referring to eternal life, the life which is God's and hence not affected by the limitations of time. **Aionios** is specially predicated on the saving blessings of divine revelation, denoting not belonging to what is transitory. Having neither beginning or end, forever, not only during the term of ones natural life time, but through endless ages of eternal life and blessedness.

Gal 1:5 to Him [be ascribed all] the glory through all the ages and the eternities of the eternities.

Definition: 3117 Yom yowm, yome from an unused root means to *be hot* a *day* (as the warm hours), lit. (from sunrise to sunset, or from one sunset to the next), today, at present, now. A point in time and a sphere of time are both express by "**yom**". **A specific point in time**. It is the **period of light** which is not darkness, in the daytime, on the same day, it can be a **period of 24 hours**, time in general, as long as, or continually. The Hebr. syn. or (216), "light", and boger (1242), "morning", are sometimes translated as "**day**". *Daytime was divided by natural phenomena*, not regular hourly divisions. The "**day**" sometimes begins with evening and sometimes with morning.

Ps 74:15, 16; *15)* You did cleave open [the rock bring forth] fountains and floods and streams; You dried up mighty, ever-flowing rivers (the Jordan): Ref. [Exod 17:6, Num 20:11, Josh 3:13]; *16)* the day is Yours, the night is Yours; You have established the light and the sun.

Definition: 1519 into eis, ice; *to* or *into* (indicating the point reached or entered) of place, time of purpose, result; implying motion into any place or thing [1525] to enter, come in, come into; [1528 & 1529] to invite in abundantly, to call in abundantly; an entrance, to rush in, entering, to hasten, run in, spring in, also a motion towards, to; until, when.

Exod. 14:**21** ***then Moses stretched out his hand over the sea; and the Lord caused the sea to go back by a strong east wind all the night and made the sea into dry land, and the waters were divided***.

Exod. 14:27 ***and Moses stretched out his hand over the sea returned and when the morning appeared, the sea returned to its full depth***. [Ref. Ps 33:7, Exod. 15:18, Heb 11:40, Job 26:11]; Josh 5: 9 ***The Lord said unto Joshua, this day have I rolled away the reproach of Egypt from off you. Wherefore the place is called Gilgal until this day***. Zech 3: 9 *For behold the stone that I have laid before Joshua; upon one stone shall be seven eyes: behold I will remove the iniquity of that land in* **one day**.

Eph. 3:21 To Him be **glory** in the church and in Christ Jesus throughout all generations or ages forever and ever. Amen (so be it). **All the generations of the age of ages** rendered "throughout all ages" or "the world without end". Dut. 7:9 ***Know, recognize, and understand therefore that the Lord your God, He is God, the faithful God. Who keeps covenant and steadfast love and mercy with those who love Him and keep His commandments, to a thousand - 1000 generations***. Dut 11:21 Your days and the days of your children **may be multiplied** in the land of which the Lord swore to your fathers to give them, ***as the days of heaven upon the earth***.

Ps 90:4 ***For a thousand years in your sight are but as yesterday when it is past or as a watch in the night or an hour of the night***.

2 Pe 3:8 But beloved, be not ignorant of this one thing, ***that one day is with the Lord as a thousand years, and thousand years as one day***. *Note!* God created time (Gen 1:1) and it is under His control (Ps 74:16) mankind must recognize the sovereignty by conforming. Exod 20:11 For in six days the Lord made the heavens and the earth, the sea, and all that is in them, and rested the seventh day. Therefore the Lord blessed the 7th or Sabbath day and hallowed it or keeping it holy; These expressions introduces events and their times particular importance in the biblical history as to the conditions of men pertains to the stages of his salvation: "**in one day** reproaches and iniquities removed" "**today** is a time of repentance", "**this day**" a time of adoption; and if not because of your rebellion you will experience the "**Day of the Lord**" as "a day of darkness", "A day of cloud and thick darkness"; Joel 2:2, Amos 5:8 "a day of famine "A day of wrath", a day of trouble and distress, a day of wastefulness and desolation and darkness and gloom. [Ref. **Zech. 14: 1, 7, 8,**]

PROMISE PHASE 3: TIME
INTERLUDE: CURSE OF FUTURE TIME

Eccl. 8:15 That which has been is now; and that which is to be hath already been and God requires that which is past.

In **Shoshana Zuboff** book 'In the age of the smart machine – The future of work and power' she helps us understand that symbolic mediums provides a distance from reality and experience which produces a thinning affect or dilution of meaning, a depravation. She quotes from Ernst Cassirer work in the Philosophy of Symbolic forms, Vol. 3 of The Phenomenology of Knowledge (New Haven: Yale University Press, 1957, p.114) when he discusses the power of the symbol to transcend the limitations of the present tense: "only where we succeed as it were in compressing a total phenomenon into one of its factors, in concentrating it symbolically, in "having" it in a state of "pregnancy" in their particular factor – only then do we raise it out of the stream of temporal change; only then does it existence, gained a permanence: for only then does it become possible to find again in the simple, as it were, punctual "here" and "now" of our present experience 'a not-here" and "a not-now". Everything that we called the…, is rooted in this fundamental act of finding again. Thus it is a common function which makes possible…specific articulation of the intuitive world.

This helps our dialect within the context of Satan's debt ridden system and its subtleness which is too complex to be made explicit. The knowledge that society has about the symbolic medium of the debt system is tacit; and therefore has become inherently evanescent in the larger, yet invisible "consumer" economy. Why is this? This larger sector of the economy has never been integrated into the profit structures of the economy but only though the medium of exchange (the now super symbolic characteristics of money) of the world financial debt base systems. The symbolic debt system is reflected in every aspect of our daily business transactions; such as the additional banking fees, price increases (gasoline, heating) and compound interest that have been subtly imposed upon society for our convenience by using their technology. But this is the model used at our expense throughout history. However, all this will become worse as the pressure builds up within Satan's close system of debt that we will discuss later.

General knowledge and know how regardless of the quantity or variety is of little use in the accumulation of money. Our great universities possess unlimited categories of general knowledge known to civilization. Unfortunately, most professors have but little money. Worse still, a larger percentage approximately

60% to 70% of their students they teach which represents the future, know little about participating in the profit structure of the capitalistic system and how it functions other than working for corporate America and being indebted to it. Even knowledge, that is organized and intelligently directed, implemented through practical plans and strategies in order to accomplish the designed objective in most cases fall short or have the same negative cash flow who results, inevitably worsens over time. This is an inherent design of the world debt system. Consequently, this has and will always continue producing the same negative, and ineffective results specifically from an economical standpoint.

Regardless of the quantity of human wisdom or the apparent quality of the world academic community and the highly educated politicians or their financial institutions and the corporations they regulate is all part of the evil plan of the small percentage of the super elites to suppress specific knowledge that would open the flood gate for wealth creation. The capitalistic system of the world must limit the larger percentage of society from participating in the profit structure of the economy or it will collapse. The super elite have been able to maximize for themselves a greater participation of the smaller business sector into its capitalistic debt system. Through our income, and earnings this produces wealth for a select few now, but an illusionary expectancy of wealth later for the larger populace. The super elites evil plans and their activities must be to perpetuate the general knowledge of debt, credit, loans, interest and their various instruments that supports the ideology of controlling their wealth by enslaving the middleclass, and neglecting the poor and poverty stricken culture because of it.

The debt system has weakened nations and continues producing highly educated fools who remains disconnected from the system while still supporting and working for the very system that impoverishes them. We can see that the suppression of knowledge concerning wealth creation has severely limited the distribution of real, workable capital among all classes. Historically, and even now, only a tiny percentage of the population has been socialized into knowledge at the level of the meta-languages of control and innovation, whereas the mass of the population has been socialized into knowledge at the level of context-tied operations. A tiny percentage of the population has been given access to the principles of intellectual change, whereas the rest has been denied such access.

However, knowing is only half the battle. Many Christians who should know the truth have instead increased in gaining worldly information. They don't understand the mysteries of the truth about the kingdom (the deep things of God and His truth) in order to apply kingdom principles secularly and then to practice its principles so as to mature in the present now. Because of this Christians seldom look within themselves for this vast field of consciousness (New Jerusalem) where the scope of the harvest is plentiful but the realization of its vastness by kingdom leaders are few. The mental activity of mind sowing and reaping is lacking and it is this reason that the white fields aren't reaped by kingdom leaders, because they don't understand how the landscape (New Jerusalem) look outside of the physical Jerusalem of the old testament. Unfortunately, civilizations as a whole and Christians specifically are frozen in time past and aren't aware of its teaching, application or that it exists presently now.

If the financial debt-credit system of the past give you an identity and the future holds the promise of your dreams; then, why is there a dizzying mental disorientation brought on by the premature arrival of it? For example, when we have a strong appetite or ardent desire for pleasing a diseased soul by acquiring the things desired though debt in advance before it is paid for. We have not only become psychological slaves to those material things acquired though the lust of the flesh but have taken on the consequences; though ownership of the instruments of debt (unjust gains though marginal investing, derivatives, PFA-plucked from the air, increasing compound interest, false balances, loan accumulations, inflation, dishonest scales of fractional reserve banking). These are the inherent results associated with any debt-credit base system and its unjust money and dishonest weights and dishonest business.

For it is the super symbolic characteristic of the debt system that project our minds into the future with the expectancy of being rewarded when we either die and our family benefit or we retire and hopefully it will be there for our golden years. The progressive projection of our minds have become locked into a false future and is compounded by driving our obsessed lives compulsively towards an impossible task of trying to satisfy a past by paying off the various schemes of the instruments of debt projected in the future.

If time is money and money has become super symbolic; then time has turn increasingly to an intangible medium of exchange for the world financial debt creation system. The policies of the governing institutions such as the SEC, and the FED are founded on this fundamental premise that underlines and governs the debt capital systems of the world. The psychological affect is intended to always keep society's thinking distracted and locked into a mind set of future time existence. However, according to **Eckhart Tolle** work "The Power of the Now" he states that "time is an illusion". Any society that is dependent on the world debt system does not understand that time past and the future are but an illusion. Eventually, this further leads to stagnation in the present-now; while frozen in time past. Until society is freed from this delusion the present-now will be misinterpreted and misunderstood. Being that the future is a subsuming synthesis and replication of the past and the endless attempts to fulfill an unsatisfied present keeps the world psychologically locked into Satan's lie which is his modus operandi.

It's impossible to see one's inheritance inside of a one dimensional mindset-unless you grasp the beauty of thinking in higher dimensions spiritually according to Christ. Like rivers of water that divides and flows through channels to irrigates the landscape of gardens, vineyards and fields so that the different cycles, courses or sequence of different commodities of crop rotations. You'll never understand that God has already moved this new information of kingdom economics, and shifted the dimension of **pre-appointed times** (the vertical and horizontal windows) from a place of eternity (the isometric 3 dimensional-cube) and historically to a place already laid up and planted in the center of men's heart, for the present now, manifestations of the business cycles and courses of kingdom economics that are held by God in the hearts of kingdom leaders are the **holy time cycles** that break up the fallow soil of mental poverty. By restoring the mind and refreshing the soul one begin to look away from the dependency of debt, credit and loans.

But the manifestation of this grand awakening within us will never happen, until we replace our tacit knowledge and forsake our past experiences with the buds of his wisdom and spiritual understanding. This process irrigates all aspects of the heart in order to bring forth a renewed harvest of his holy time cycles. Likewise, we will continue to wonder in the wilderness, based on the same effects of the world system that is constantly sapping value and quality of life from our life and wondering why our preconditioned lives, our settled comfort zones, and financial state is worsening. We are conscious that something is wrong but have become powerless to do any thing about it. This is the debt system that majority of society is disconnected from; however, while at the same time enslaved and dependant on it.

The irony behind Jesus demonstrations was that then our promises and blessings had been already proven by God though the generations of Abraham and his lineage eons ago; this however, seems far fetch when compared to the lack of limited manifestations of Gods overcoming blessings in today's' religious communities. Even as Christians we can't even fathom the manifold promises and blessings that have been so prevalent and abundant during that agriculture period of Jesus time, that in most cases was taken for granted just as debt today is taken for granted. When God's blessings seem to have rained upon every living thing including the land where various harvests cycles (grain, fruit, vegetable, livestock, etc.) occurred simultaneously in various seasons throughout the year.

All of this rich heritage of abundant sowing and reaping was part of everyday life and in most cases then must have been taken for granted. But though history we've slowly been separated from this rich heritage of ours by the introduction of usury. Where have all of the overcoming blessings and the covenant promises that we should be experiencing at a higher level today all gone to? Why aren't these same blessings that are promised to us manifested as it was then today?

Unfortunately, for the most part kingdom leaders can't see or think outside of the ordinary limits of their consciousness as a result of tradition; because unknowingly, they are stuck in the physical scope of lust and the insatiable appetites for the accumulation of material possessions. Most of our worldly possessions are attained by borrowing through the debt base system of credit, and high interest rates. Christians specifically and society as a whole have become locked into a two dimensional way of thinking and teaching. Worse still the evil activities generates one dimensional results designed to enslave God's people to the debt system of this world.

History will always repeat itself because there is nothing new under the sun. In **Fernand Braudel** research, he describes in his book: Civilization and Capitalism 15th and 18th century: The Structures of Everyday Life; "the shadowy zone …one finds that active social hierarchies (pyramids) were constructed on top of it: they create anomalies, zones of turbulence and conducted their affairs in a very individual way. At this exalted level, a few wealthy merchants in the eighteenth century Amsterdam or sixteenth-century Geno – could throw whole sectors of Europe or world economy into confusion, from a distant". Certain groups of privileged actors were engaged in circuits and calculations that ordinary people knew nothing of…was tied to distant trade movements and to the complicated arrangements for credit, was a sophisticated art, open only to a few initiators at most."

The bonds of money and the market did not encompass all human life. The poor chose to evade it. It was possible to say in about 1713, that variations in money hardly interest the greater part of the peasants (in Burgundy) who do not possess currency. This was true almost always for peasants everywhere." The general public found this type of money (Satan's IOU- debt system) that really wasn't money at all but the symbolism of it, to be more of an imposition than a benefit. Therefore, real wealth was replaced by symbolic wealth or illusionary wealth. That's why in the shadowy world of credit and debt it seemed very diabolical and was very difficult to understand then as it is today. Why? Because throughout history capital moved by stages from tangible money to an intangible symbolism of money and capital which is of course attached to the sin of debt. This type of sin keeps society missing the mark of God's purpose for man to help prevent him from stumbling and falling.

Now super symbolic money must be perceived intuitively out side of tangible money. There is an inherent disconnect associated with debt capital and the production of its debt instruments. The production of these instruments is a direct result of society's insatiable appetite for credit; driven by instant gratification it is built into the very fabric of our everyday life activities that we can't do without. The symbolic aspect of all money (derivatives, indexes and all of its instruments) is debt. Debt is too evasive and complex for the majority of society to comprehensively understand. Even the experts are under enormous pressure in their feeble attempts to reform all of the various entitlement programs that have been in disarray for centuries are beyond repair.

From a historical perspective you can understand why the problems of today could only be solved through the expansion of the debt system. Through the research of **Alvin Toffler** in his work The Third Wave and Power Shift has revealed the affects of the "invisible wedge" (industrial revolution upon the "invisible market") from allowing the CM (consumer market) from participating in the profit structure of the debt system. The backlash of the invisible wedge are creating economic pressures that are forcing a paradigm shift with the powers that be and the BM (business market) as it relates to creating and enlarging more false wealth internationally; while at the same time, opening the flood to then the unseen potential for greater debt creation infused into the larger CM (consumer market).

In 1519, during the agriculture era, 90% of the larger underdeveloped population the CM lived on the soil producing only a small amount of goods for trade in the BM. Of that more than 70% never enter the smaller economy of the elite capitalist of the Mediterranean business markets. The economy of BM was industrialized for profit and move in the undeveloped economy of CM like a whirlwind. However, because the larger sectors of the CM were transparent to the smaller economy of the BM 70% of the larger markets will never enter the smaller economy of the BM. That's like trying to put 100 pounds of potatoes inside of a one pound potato sack. The smaller market of the BM can't support the larger CM it would burst open if it tried. Debt used to be geared for the investors of smaller sector, but is now being designed to transition with open arms to the general public.

OWNERSHIP SOCIETY
Slavery vs. Entitlement

This extraordinary truth applies specifically to the entitlement programs (pensions, retirement and social security) that are non-employable, non-working money accumulated for hoarding. Over time social security, 401k and retirement have become increasingly insecure property for those dependent on it; but if wealth is founded in property then society have become enslaved by the false accumulation of it. The danger arose when the real owners abused this property by the depreciation of it, which they never plan to make up for. Historically, back in 1865 blacks were in a similar situation when President Andrew Johnson ordered land to be returned to its former owners. Blacks expected the federal government to provide farm land that they felt they were entitled to, justifiably so based on their past labors and contributions.

The transitional progression of the debt system doesn't just affect blacks then; but today society's future as a whole is threatened if and when their entitlements are taken away by the transposition, will especially effects those who life depends directly on entitlements and the diminishing affects debt has had upon its long term equity; thereby, destroying the equality of the property that has been set aside for society.

In comparison and from an economic standpoint, the work of Eric Foner "Reconstruction: America's Unfinished Revolution" points to the same conditions that existed when one see similar parallels from time past in relations to the split on slavery during the civil war. The northerners or Republicans who didn't own many slaves nor slaves territory was the minority of the two parties but was more economically diversified with foreign bankers, merchants, manufacturers demonstrating that trade, commerce, banking and shipping could be equally if not more profitable and rewarding than slavery.

However, the southern/democrats who own the majority of slave territory and the slave producing commercial crops, their staples and expansion of slave territory was more attached to the slave institution. This severely limited their economic opportunity for growth and their inability to shift with the changing climate (The Civil Wars, The New Deals, free slave movement, The Emancipation Proclamation, The Reconstruction era, The American Revolution) during the political or economical transitions made them more attached.

The base of slave institution of the south gradually eroded. The Democrats could not sustain economic diversity and social development for their black slaves, because they continue lagging farther behind as the economic shift occur.

We are witnessing the same conditions in the 21st century as the Democrat and all of society finds themselves especially African Americans in the conditions now as they were then in the late 17th century left behind of change.

The irony behind the dichotomy is astonishingly perplexing. Here again, it shows the historical and present parallels when looking at the root of this type of separation and the emphases placed on the conflicting economic interest of the halves. This condition have placed society specifically African Americans alone with other ethnic affiliations in the middle of an ever widening economic gulf; with slavery being the root cause then and its entitlements being the root causes today domestically other than war. The economic duality of any analogous relationship must be **reciprocated** regardless of any relative limiting factor. On one hand the larger percentage of society is comfortable relying on their failing entitlement program; even when the fact shows the dyer need for reform it will still be contrary to the justification of their dependency to it; while at the same time, inevitably being forced to migrate to the more risky aspects of the capitalistic system, as entitlements are slowly **transitioned** into the funded system of personal accounts.

Here is another historical parallel whereby the agricultural industry was **transposed** into the industrial revolution and so on into the present state the information age. Usury had to transmute accordingly and attach itself to these **transitional** periods throughout the ever evolving history of the ages.

Reluctantly; and with much vituperations the political atmosphere of our leaders and society had to change accordingly, even to their own or others destruction. Rather society change or not the irrefutable effects of the **transition** are caused by the agencies of **usury** concealed between the various **dichotomies** and without them ever being identified; their influential affects will only precipitate our inadvertent acceptance of them during their transition.

So the transition of revenues will of course include a long drawn out process that will take time for society to adapt to; but inevitably, entitlement reform will be introduce to the capital market as **circulating capital** with interest, **transitional** cost attached to it. The prerequisite for this to happen will entail the **transformation** of bureaucracy along with opening to some degree the integration of two closed worlds. **Transforming** the social-economics diversity of the larger economy by giving it access to the maximizing capacities of the debt system for social advancement is attempting the impossible, by forbidding money from being multiplied. Money can't be dismantled and then retreat backward, it is the instruments of exchange for which all economies progress with.

The extraordinary truth about entitlements, as difficult as it might be to accept is that they are not our possession until we take ownership of it; which is usually over a certain age and after a certain period of time of service. The debt/ credit machine must increase profit by putting stagnate money into circulation entitlements included. In one way or another, money must be constantly rejoined and mingled in the main stream of monetary circulation. This occurs when the value of the entitlement has been depleted or depreciated. The whole system must be reproduced and repackaged into a perpetual profit funded system. When worn out method of borrowing is restricted or cash runs low, or the retirement age is raised hoarding occurs.

Adaptability of capitalism

Under these insurmountable economic pressures and as difficult as it might be to justify, all the entitlements systems non circulated capital will succumb to these pressures and must eventually be injected into the investment market. This is an essential feature of capitalistic adaptability to change and the unlimited flexibility to shift at a moment's notice – which covers a multitude of forms from one form or section to another; in times of crisis even if the new sources of revenue entitlement is earmarked. The accumulation of revenues (entitlements) although justified, are becoming relics of the past; primarily because those huge money pools are static and aren't circulated as capital for use in the industry especially during a time of war when government must mobilize all the nations resources including the reservoirs of large sums of money that's untapped or lying idle; rather it be their own or other people's money.

Based on the historical patterns of the political leadership there is every indication that an ominous revolutionary transformation will occur, based on increased pressure to produce more debt capital for the debt system. One possible hypothesis that is under strong consideration and will eventually become a reality long after the introduction of president G.W. Bush propose reformation of the personal accounts though the repackaged hybrid scheme of the 'ownership society' program. The purpose is to maximize all business variables by leveraging more debt instruments outside of the smaller economy into the larger invisible economy. This is the same debt pattern that has operated under the radar at speeds unimaginable to the general public. Against great resistance the entitlements will be more vulnerable when the new debt creation model of the "ownership society is transformed and magnified into a greater **closed debt- loop** system because the knowledge will remain mostly tacit to the hoarding, bureaucratic elitist who constrains the super symbolic medium of debt money; however, all this is about to change as financial and political pressure within the debt system heat up and forces changes in the monetary policy.

The attempts to reform these entitlement programs are rare and have provoked the loudest outcry specifically from the democrats and controversial complaints against some other 150 proposed necessary cuts by the Republican Party to reduce federal spending. The out cry of these ill feelings has lain dormant since 1935. Today, these ill feelings are the results of the unwillingness of our culture to accept the need for change; in addition to the lack of political leadership needed to develop serious reform to the antiquated entitlement programs. The social security program was created during the depression. The saving and loan fiasco created the 401k system or the now debunked pension system and debased retirement plans that exist today. In the near future, the relentless push to legislate (PA) personal accounts though the concept of *"ownership society"* extends the debt system to replenish the depleted money supplies of the pension and retirement funds. Although there is great resistance to this ideology by Congress, regulators, and, special interest groups it must first evolve into an accepted legitimized policy. In fact it has already been approved because it is the largest privately held corporation – the Federal Reserve Bank (the Fed) and it control the monetary policy not congress. So the concern should be not when, but what financial crisis will it take to subsume the personal accounts into the consumer market. The ideology of repackaging the debt structure is design to pass on the burdens of the debt system on to the already bent over backs of the consumer just as the savings and loan crisis did to 10s of millions of homeowners.

In **James Wardner** work 'The planned destruction of America' show how Congress have rendered control of the monetary system under relentless pressure from the banking institutions. Over time, the door to Pandora's Box will be opened to all types of abuses: (fraud, hoarding, greed from governments and corporations). The invisible society that is slowly being integrated into what is now called the **"ownership society"** is another repackaged scheme for personal accounts; whereby, a portion of the fiscal responsibility of government is being shifted from the investor to the individual to invest a percentage of their income back into the same system that plucked the money away from them originally. This will create an enormous amount of illusionary wealth for the individual investor, and those that is employed long term. But for the government and financial institutions an enormous amount of wealth will be produced immediately for them.

Freedom through God's Time

Freeing the larger populace of society requires an understanding of God's time. But outside of this, the whole world has been exposed to the schemes and practices of **usury**. In society through the secular use of **usury**, time has become unfortunately an unconscious dimension of human life used as an intangible tool for **false wealth creation** through the debt system. However, before usury, time belong to God alone and still does; but to sell it as man has (in the many forms of interest) was to sell what did not belong to them. And as a result, kingdom leaders aren't aware that it is an obstacle for entering into higher levels of salvation, as heirs having authority and ownership over God's holy time cycles. But now, that man is in possession of time and is controlled by it through the debt system he has become a slave to the sin of usury. This delusion has enslaved the world leaders of society to a seemingly inescapable system postponing the true reality of wealth for the masses of the world that could be theirs if they only understood the alternative to this world debt system through kingdom economics.

At this time kingdom leaders cannot afford the cost of being lackadaisical which destroys and hardens the human spirit preventing the majority of society from becoming enterprising. The generational cycles of laxity in relations to true leadership development is not continuously being communicated through financial deeds of prudence reflected in kingdom lifestyles; but is more so now the continuous overindulgence in vituperative demagoguery and the plausibility of leadership. Unknowingly, many political leaders that fall under these dogmatic conditions are not prepared to lead and deal with the overwhelming responsibility of creating false wealth through the debt system and shouldn't be expected to. So, any leadership who chooses to lead and have not developed the financial astuteness; especially within a system or economy laden with the inter-cyclical depressions the debt system produces, makes it very difficult and even futile for them to produce real economic opportunity through wealth distribution in which their support system the government can't do. But there is a better way to overcome this seemingly inescapable system by spiritually recognizing the only biblical strategy that promises to bless your life today.

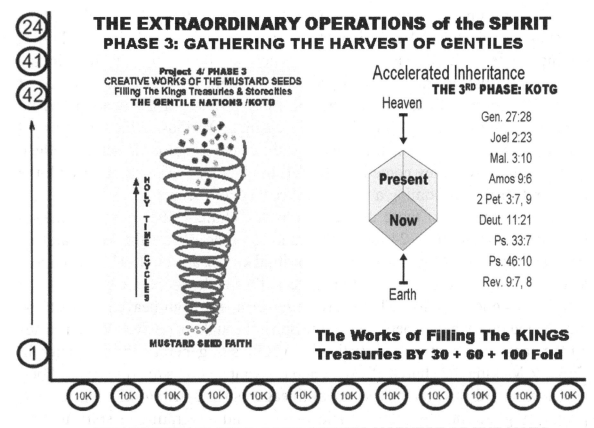

Figure 9

FIGURE 9 GRAPH EXPLANATION

Circle 24 in this figure is the submitted aspect of the church (then, where the 24 elders of the priesthood performed their 24 courses or cycles of service throughout the 12 tribes) to the kingship (KOTK-H) circle 41 along with the gentile (KOTG) nations of the world circles 42. All consummated within circle 1, completing and making up the DNA of Christ. The true priesthood today should be serving both, through the operations of the spirit and through the power of the king's office then, that this power can today be transitioned into higher levels of wealth demonstrations through all applicable spiritual kingships. And as a result into the spiritual kingship; and by decree, they automatically become a subsume entity into a higher class of royal authority and integrated into a larger inheritance, inheriting the 12 tribes, the promises and service to the gentile nations. This action is indicated by the removal of the 12 horizontal circles that has the # 1's in them. To see the enclosed box condition of the church prior to its submission and transition reference *figures 2, 5 and 7*. The church by this

132

one divine act opens up the gentile nations to the true spiritual kingship and the priest line of Melchizedek allowing it to operate outside of its religious traditions. Giving the transposed church (circle 24); now as the multiplicity of spiritual kings, the transformed entity can progress through the transitional phases of both POI-process of integration and the POD-process of duplication having greater access to the king's promises and blessings. Obviously, this is the perfect kingdom scenario; only then, if the kingship of the kingdom is acknowledged by the church, will they come into the full implications of integrating with the DNA of Christ in becoming a world wide reality for them.

The progression of these divine acts by the churches has now become all inclusive through circle 24 being the church, circle 41 are the kings and its kingdom leadership (the multiplicity of spiritual kings), and circle 42 is the nation, again all 3 entities consummated in circle 1. This is the prophetic blueprint and activity designed to allow Christ, divine government from heaven above to be manifested through the operations of the Spirit throughout circle 1. Which closes all the gaps and be integrated vertically to 1000's of generations as depicted in *figure 9*. Making the church effective and relevant again as the royal priesthood and now united with the eternal royal lineage as the spiritual kings of Christ; [connecting the church to the 7 vertical circles and integrating its spirit into all the various dynamic kingdom structures: [(the 2 in 1 in Christ, the 12 disciples in Christ, the 24 priest in Christ, the 144,000 multiplicity of spiritual kings and their kingdom leadership in Christ, the 10,000's(10k) x 10,000's(10k) + 1,000(1k) x 1000(1k) nations in Christ, etc.)], as indicated in all the graphs and *figures* when combined. Once the transition of all 3 promise phases (one of unity for the the multiplicity of spiritual kings KOTK-H, two of works operations of the Spirit KOTP, and three the acceleration of the times of the KOTG / nations) are consummated within phase 4, then a greater magnification of divine intensity is created continuously within circle 41 indicated in *figure 3*. It is these continuous processes that accelerates our inheritance (the 30, 60, and 100 fold harvest which includes our overcoming promises and manifold blessings) throughout all 3 phases completing the POI-process of integration within circles 41.

We now come full circle to promise phase 4 being the totality of all 3 phases. The culmination within circle 41 has within its POI, the multitudinous effects, that when superimposed upon circle 42 is magnified into infinite manifestations together with the POD also within circle 42. These new correlative combinations of both the POI and POD now accelerates the transitional processes of wealth redistribution into higher levels of acceleration for the kingdom leadership. The redistribution of wealth which flows ubiquitously through all *9 figures* of the kingdom economic system is the 1st phase of the spiritual king line of Christ, but immediately becomes magnified as the 4th phase of redistributed wealth for the entire DNA of Christ.

How do the earth be made to give birth of a "white field harvest" at once? We don't live in the agricultural era any longer. If the harvest is already here, then why wait four months until the harvest come? If it's here, then where is the harvest at? We don't live on farms today I don't own a farm, where is our 40 acres and our mules. How would you like to have for yourself 1000 hours in a day? Is this get rich quick? These and many other questions can seem quite confusing to the blind leaving one ignorant about their kingly heritage from a biblical perspective! But if you come to understand that the earth is the Lord's and it is full of His riches, and out of the riches of His wealth, He gives to you the glorious riches of His treasuries. God can provide you with all of your needs. Thereby, removing the iniquity and reproach or any other cares you may have or even think of having, because one day with Christ is like a 1000 years.

Jesus appearing is now superimposed today in Christ, who is Lord of the white field harvest; opening up the windows of heaven to dispense through the entire remnant seeds of the KOTK-H (circle 41) and pouring out a one day blessing upon the KOTG (circle 42) indicative to phase 3 of this figure. He is waiting to discharge His blessings, from its heavenly confinement, upon His spiritual kings and the kingdom leadership (the multiplicity of spiritual kings) and the nations of the world that continues to integrate into the DNA of Christ. Historically, Christ has at certain times transcends the chronological system of time to produce special economic activities through His spiritual kings today which at different times becomes a ubiquitous phenomenon, that's magnified across all 12 circles horizontally and vertically through 1000's of generations. While simultaneously magnifying Himself throughout tens of billions (10,000,000,000) of structured circles according to the DNA of Christ, as circle 41 continue to glorify and magnify itself within circle 42. It is at this point that the KOTK-H is ubiquitously magnified throughout the entire DNA of Christ.

At appointed times Christ leaps over to accelerate the fullness or filling up the times of the Gentiles (KOTG), in order to raise their foundations across many generations. He has also extended His heavenly treasure trove to the nations; thereby, enriching and reestablishing their treasured cities and store houses; by acting as unlimited treasuries, they also become depositories for copious deposits of redistributed wealth. The kingdom wealth of God's economy; as wealth redistribution are hidden channels of liquidity and must first be redistributed to the spiritual kings (heirs and joint heirs) of today, and eventually administered through them to the great multitudes of many nations in the earth as if heaven is on earth. That which has been will be done and what will be is now already done; because God requires it today what has been done in the past!

The eternal purpose of God is for His spiritual kings to proclaim and implement the kingdom blueprint by fusing together this gulf of ignorance, where Christ fills these gaps up with all of our diverse promises and manifold blessings; thereby, closing the gaps of disconnects. Now, we spiritual kings can leap over the divides to become the medium, through which, Christ can delegate authority to the multitudes of nations, who are now the heirs to administer God's kingdom wealth. This is the manifest expression of the true essence of kingdom economics; to become a ubiquitous channel (as bases of operations for storehouses) for wealth redistribution. We have unveiled what was once laid up in abeyance, but is now known by its rightful heirs. We now hold the keys of wisdom to unlock these hidden dimensions of God's treasure trove of wealth in the secret places of His chamber and treasuries.

Today, this ubiquitous phenomenon are the perpetual acceleration of our business cycles or holy time cycles that fills our treasuries at appointed times. First, with the munificent promises of our 30 and 60 fold harvests distributed throughout phase 1; which is then, consummated with our manifold blessings of our 100 fold harvest from phase 3. The economic magnitude equates financially to a divine compensation package of a 10,000% payout indicative to phase 1 and phase 3 shown in *figures 4 or 7.* Today the business cycles that is inherent to this type of kingdom system can be looked upon in comparison to the copious seasonal cycle in relations to the historical 7 harvest feasts relative to the "white field harvest" rather it came through the biblical examples of Joseph (producing salvation to Jacob during the famine of Egypt), Joshua (allotting or possession of inheritance to the 12 tribes), or what Jesus had immediately produced for His 12 disciples then. These kingdom economic examples still exist for the spiritual kings to produce an even greater demonstration as Christ's spiritual leadership for the glory of God, His Son and us His heirs.

The Kingdom of the Gentiles:Predestination of Glory

3rd Phase: 100 Fold Cycle Harvest

Rom 15:16 In making me a minister of Christ Jesus to the **Gentiles**. In ministering the gospel [Good news] of God, in order that the sacrificial offering of the Gentiles may be acceptable to God, consecrated and made holy by the Holy Spirit.

*Ps 110:3 Your **people** will offer themselves willingly in the day of your power, in the beauty of holiness and in holy array out of the womb of the morning; to you [will spring forth] your **young men**, who are as the dew.*

Phil 3:13, 14; 13) I do not consider, brethren, that I have captured and made it my own [yet]; but one thing I do [it is my one aspiration]: forgetting what lies behind and straining forward to what lies ahead. 14)I press on toward the goal to win the [supreme and heavenly] prize to which God in Christ Jesus is calling us upward. Col 1:28, 29; Whom we preach, warning every man, and teaching every man in all wisdom; that we may present every man perfect in Christ. For this I labor [unto weariness] striving with all the human energy which He so mightily enkindles and works within me.

Is 60:5 *Then thou shall see, and flow together and be radiant, and your heart shall thrill and tremble with joy [at the glorious deliverance] and be enlarged; because the abundant wealth of the Dead Sea shall be turned to you, unto you shall the nations come with their treasures.* Is 60:22 *A little one shall become a thousand and a small one a strong nation. I the Lord will hasten it in its time.*

Is 65:8, 9; Thus says the Lord: *As the juice [of the grape] is found in the cluster, and one says, do not destroy it, for there is a blessing in it, so will I do for my servants' sake, that I may not destroy them all. And I will bring forth an offspring from Jacob, and from Judah an inheritor of My mountains; My chosen and elect will inherit it, and My servants will dwell there.*

*Rom 9:6-8; But it is not that the Word of God has taken no effect. For the Jews are not all Israel who are of Israel. 7) Nor are they all children because they are the seed of Abraham; but Isaac your seed shall be **called**. 8) Those who are children of the flesh these are not the children of God; but the children of the promise are counted as the seed.*

Mic 5:7, 8 *Then the remnant of Jacob shall be in the midst of many peoples like dew from the Lord, like showers upon the grass which [came suddenly*

136

appearing] among the flocks of sheep which, when it goes through, treads down and tears in pieces, and there is no deliverer.

Dut 7:7, 9 The Lord did not set His love upon you and choose you because you were more in number than any other people, for you were the fewest of all people. Know, recognize, and understand therefore that the Lord your God, He is God, the faithful God, who keeps covenant and steadfast love and mercy with those who love Him and keep His commandments, **to a thousand generations**.

Is 58:12 And they that shall be of thee shall build the old waste places: **thou shalt raise up the foundations of many generations;** Gen 17:6, 7 And I will make you exceedingly fruitful and I will make nations of you, and kings will come from you. And I will establish My covenant between Me and you and your descendants after you throughout their generations for an everlasting, solemn pledge, to be a God to you and to your posterity after you.

Is 11:11, 12; 11)And in that day the Lord shall again lift up His hand a second time to recover, **acquire and deliver** the **remnant** of His people which is left, from Assyria, from Lower Egypt, from Pathros, from Hamath [in Upper Syria], and from the countries bordering on the [Mediterranean] Sea. 12) And He will raise up a signal for the nations and will assemble the **outcast of Israel** and will gather together the dispersed of Judah from the four (4) corners of the earth.

Eph 2:14-16; *14)* For He is [Himself] our peace (*our bond of unity and harmony). He has made us both [Jew and Gentile] one [body], and has broken down (destroyed, abolished) the hostile dividing wall between us. 15) By abolishing in His [own crucified] flesh the enmity [caused by] the Law with its decrees and ordinances [which He annulled]; that He from the two might create in Himself one new man [one new quality of humanity out of the two], so making peace. 16) And [He designed] to reconcile to God both [Jew and Gentile, united] in a single body* by means of His cross, thereby killing the mutual enmity and bringing the feud to an end.

Rev 5:5, 6, 9-12; *5)* But one of the elders said to me, do not weep. *Behold the Lion of the tribe of Judah, the Root of David, has prevailed* to open the scroll and to loose its seven seals. *6) And I looked, and behold in the midst of the throne and of the four living creatures, and in the midst of the elders, stood a Lamb as though it had been slain, having seven horns and seven eyes, which the seven (7) Spirits of God are sent out into all the earth.*

9) And the saints sang a new song…for you were slain, and have redeemed us to God by His blood out of every tribe and tongue and people and nation. 10) And have made us kings and priest to our God; and we shall reign on the earth. **11*) Then I looked, and I heard the voice of many angels around the throne,***

the twelve (12) living creatures, and the twelve (12) elders; and the number of them was(10,000) ten-thousand times (10,000) ten-thousand, and (1000) thousands of (1000) thousands.

Jesus Answer to Kingdom Ascendancy

How then can society escape the inescapable forces of this immaterial medium of exchange and the ingenious practice of **usury, interest and debt** by the elite that are part of our every day life? There are two suggestions and only one is the solution. In Luke 4: 5, 6 – Jesus in a moment of time **turn down the devil's kingdom and his world system of debt.** This is the very system the powerful elites have come to accept, the illusionary deception of wealth creation. A capitalist machine that serves the vigilant interest of the worldly rich, this system will be served by those who wish to either prosper from it or suffer by it. However, to prosper or not, it offers a progressive decline that will worsen before it gets better.

One cannot help but laugh at the ironic humor when the devil showed **Jesus** his kingdom **'in a moment of time'** very quickly in hopes that **Jesus** would not see the devastation Satan's system produces upon the people of the world. Nevertheless, Satan's offered to give Jesus **power and glory** from his kingdom that hadn't any. This radical and promising view of Satan's opportunity didn't impress nor astonish Jesus at all, as the inhabitants of the world has become, with all of its confusion and perplexities and broking promises. Even the church tried to grapple with the debt system and eventually succumbed to the relentless debate that goes back centuries to the ancient times of Deuteronomy and the **church** prohibition against usury. Here you have it, the choice between two kingdoms, Satan's kingdom that's lived and seen, while Jesus kingdom was rejected because it was not seen; therefore, not lived and waited for; because the former kingdom was the people choice. This choice gave occasion at that moment for Satan's underlying lie and all of his destructive consequences to remain effective.

If you were to tell someone that they were a **king** they would probably look at you real strange and ask what am I a **king** over? Heck, I don't even vote! In the western culture there are no longer kingdoms, and therefore no **kings** to rule them. It is the public that's sovereign in our democratic republic today, and we the people choose a president and other representatives in the Senate and house; supposedly, with the whole process governed by the Constitution of the United States. A constitution which was founded on Godly principles: in God we trust, one nation under God, prayer in schools, God bless America, etc. and looking at all the encroachments upon these principles are tearing away the fabric of society.

However, in our system and culture today, it is the political leadership who is more interested in being politically correct and consequently, by default, must change the laws more to appease the **public** who have strayed away from their authority and responsibility as sovereign. Compound this by the evil influences of corporate America on society seemed to have made what's right wrong and what's wrong right. The further the political leadership got away from these principles and the word of God, the more control we have relinquished to Satan; who even back then, attempted to influence the LORD of Lords and **KING OF KINGS**, the King of glory.

But little did Satan know, **Jesus Christ** was already victorious in overcoming the world. Satan was already defeated, and placed under Jesus feet. Unknown to Satan (the Lunatic) Jesus kingdom was already at hand; because in his **present now, then "it has already been said, and it was already written"**. The word of promise, that **Christ** the humiliated is the ruler over the kingdom of heaven. He has already overcome Satan's world, since from the beginning, being the only begotten, Jesus had already pre-existed and came from above then; but is now, not only, sat down on His own throne; but is also sat at His Father right hand within His Father throne. What a beautiful, mental picture of our heavenly heritage in the minds of those who place their hope and anticipation in. In **Christ's** circle (of alpha and omega, the 1st and last, the beginning and ending) and through his promises, this generation as **heirs to Christ promises** of all things is at hand for us (the children of the promise) to overcome the world-Satan's kingdom, as kings in the earth as he did! We are brought forth from darkness and isolation, from being separated and "called out" we have become exalted and made **kings** and priests. It was then, when Jesus appointed to us our **kingdom**, we can now rule as **kings** through the heavenly sphere that springs from **Christ kingdom** in the republic. In our heavenly calling, we now possess the right hand of power to overcome, that power which comes from on high; flowing through us according to His own will. He possesses all the divine authority and strength both in heaven and through us on the earth. This sovereignty and authority is the completion of the promises of our circles.

THE END

Printed in the United States
By Bookmasters